# LISTEN TO WHAT STUDENTS SAY

## A COLLEGE SUCCESS GUIDE

### CARMY CARRANZA
Indiana University of Pennsylvania

**KENDALL/HUNT PUBLISHING COMPANY**
4050 Westmark Drive        Dubuque, Iowa 52002

# DEDICATION

This book is dedicated to my inspirations:
José
Paul
Erica
Mary
Jim
and
Jimmy

# CONTENTS

# PREFACE

The material for this book was taken from a study about student success. The quotations on the following pages were extracted from interviews with sixteen students who were enrolled in one of seven different four-year colleges or universities of varying sizes, types, and settings. As participants in the study, students were asked to talk about the factors that they believed to be important to success in college. Two particulars make their perceptions noteworthy:

- They themselves were all successful students. As they speak, each student is just days or weeks away from graduating and receiving a college degree.

- As entering freshmen, none of these students was expected to succeed. Each was admitted to college as an "at-risk" student, a student for whom the standard measures of success had predicted failure, and each had been required to participate in a support program.

Because these two conditions were the sole qualifications for including a student in the study, it was surprising to see how many of those students who were selected had also distinguished themselves in some fashion. This finding is especially noteworthy given their low prediction for college success and graduation.

For example, two of the students were graduating with honors. One of the students held an important position in student government and was also senior class president. One was on a faculty search committee, and another was a member and chair of the judicial board. Three students were paraprofessional peer-helpers and two had been nominated to speak at commencement. One student held positions on several university boards; several were regular spokespersons for their developmental program, and several held positions of leadership in academic and social organizations.

In addition, more than three fourths of the group had plans to continue with their education after graduation, underscoring further their ability to demonstrate success with the college experience. Fourteen of the sixteen students in the study were planning to attend graduate school or law school, each already having made application or specific plans, eager to be launched on another successful educational experience.

What these students have to say about the influences on their success is to be taken seriously. After all, not all "at-risk" students are successful no matter how much support they may have received. Indeed, even students whose predictions for success are highly positive will not all be successful. What makes the difference? *Listen to what students say.*

# ACKNOWLEDGMENTS

I am immensely grateful to all the students who participated in this project and who willingly allowed me into their lives, giving me more than just a glimpse of their knowledge, wisdom, and genuineness.

# NOTES ABOUT THE STRUCTURE OF THE BOOK

## TO THE INSTRUCTOR:

The following pages may be used alone or as a supplement to another text for any course that introduces students to the college experience, such as an orientation course or freshman seminar course. The text may also be used as a supplement to a college text for any of the courses typically taught in developmental or college support programs, such as courses in college reading and writing, learning strategies, or career exploration.

Instructors should find the material to be of interest to students, especially for first or second year students for whom peer influence may hold considerable sway. Instructors should find adequate flexibility to design their own assignments based on the students' readings or may use the suggestions found in the sections called *Points to Ponder* for class discussion, group work, journal entries, or writing assignments.

To encourage students to think and write about the topics and ideas presented in each chapter, a spiral bound journal is available and can be purchased along with the text. The journal may be used as a workbook with assignments extracted and turned in for credit as the instructor directs. Or it may be used strictly as a journal, wherein the students keep a running account of their thoughts, ideas, and/or assignments that may or may not be "corrected" by the instructor.

Instructors may want to remind students that because they are reading the transcripts of interviews, the students' words are representations of spoken language, not written language. The excerpts are fine examples of how journal writing may read, but for other assignments, you may expect more formal writing—and here may be a good opportunity to discuss the difference.

The text is divided into twenty-seven short chapters, each dealing with a different topic on the subject of factors in success as perceived by those students interviewed for a research study. Each chapter stands alone; therefore, there is considerable flexibility for picking and choosing those deemed most appropriate for a given class. However, chapters 3 through 9 deal with the essential factor of goals and goal commitment and are recommended reading for every class.

Chapter fourteen, *Developmental Program Support and the Precollege Summer Experience,* describes students' responses to the support they experienced as participants in programs for at-risk students. This chapter is highly recommended for students who are part of such a program, and also has applicability to other students. In this chapter, there are assignments and suggestions under *Points to Ponder* designed for both groups—those who are participating in a support program as well as those who are not. Chapter 20, *Difficulties for Minorities,* also speaks about a specific group of students, but is a topic that has relevancy for any reader.

For instructors who would like a more in-depth presentation of the research results on which this text was based may acquire the study, *Developmental Students Perceptions of the Factors That Contribute to Academic Success,* UMI, Ann Arbor, MI. For ordering the full dissertation, use catalogue #9904082, volume issue 59-08A, page 2878. This study also includes recommendations for further research and implications for program and course development. As such, this text, as well as the full study, can have special relevance for graduate courses and programs that seek to prepare developmental educators.

It is recommended that the instructor read the following section written *To the Student* for additional ideas on the use of the text and its accompanying journal and that students be required to read this section before proceeding.


## TO THE STUDENT:

Everyone talks about the effects of peer influence on young people, even on college students, maybe even ESPECIALLY on college students, where most young adults are faced for the first time with issues of separation and identity. The truth is that EVERYONE is influenced to some extent by the words and actions of his or her peers. It is a natural phenomenon. In the following pages, you will have an opportunity to hear what your college peers have to say about the topic of success in college. What you do with this influence will be up to you. The important thing is that you think about their words, compare what they have to say to your own experience, and to consider what relevance their words have to you.

To help you with that process, a spiral bound journal can be purchased along with this text or may be required by your instructor. It is recommended that you use the writing as a means of reflection and revelation. In this way, journal writing can be a powerful tool for personal growth.

The questions and suggestions found in the sections under *Points to Ponder* might be used as stimuli for your writing. Or you may choose to reflect on some topic, discussion, or activity from any of your classes, making connections and associations among ideas, looking for relevance to your own experiences, and finally, considering some implications for yourself and even beyond. In other words, you may take the approach to each of your entries where you ask yourself the questions, *What, So What, Now What?* Or your instructor may give you specific writing assignments for your journal entries.

Finally, you may want to keep your journal as an ongoing record of your growth as a learner, using it throughout your college career, and tracking your development, much as the students in this study have done with their own reflections on why they have been successful. Where the textbook gives you an opportunity to *Listen to What Students Say*, the journal gives you an opportunity to *Listen to What YOU Say.* The ultimate goal is your own personal and academic development, which, ultimately, will lead to your own success.

## The Definition of Academic Success                    Chapter 1

---

## Introduction

The students who participated in the study from which this book was created were finishing their last semester of college and preparing to receive a college degree. As graduating seniors, they had successfully completed the college experience. They had been able to accomplish what was expected of college students—to graduate. By this most basic standard measure, they had achieved academic success.

The purpose of the study was to learn something about what factors students themselves believe helped them to achieve that success. By asking students themselves to address the topic, it was expected that a deeper, more in-depth understanding of college success could emerge, especially given that none of these students had been expected to succeed in the first place. They had all been considered "at-risk" for success. The predictions that had been made about their potential for academic achievement in the college environment had been below the academic good standing required to persist. And although they had been provided with a program of support during the first year of college, others with that same support had not been able to realize the same successful outcome. Nor had others in their class—students who had begun their college experience with a far better prediction for success, or were not considered to be at-risk. What made the difference? Listen to what students say. The excerpts you will read in the following chapters have been extracted from the taped interviews in which students discussed the basic question: Why have you been successful?

Before students were asked to give their explanations, descriptions, and interpretations of factors contributing to academic success in college, they were asked to provide their own personal definition of academic success. Their responses were all quite similar. They tended to downplay the focus on grades, emphasizing, instead, the learning process, personal satisfaction, doing one's best, and maintaining balance. In other words, students at this stage were more likely to value education as a process of intellectual and personal growth and development rather than just as a means of vocational development.

Speaking of which . . .

*I would say it is not only just what grades you get. I think it is more that you care about your education. Not just whether I get an A, but if I got something out of the class.*

*I think success is just being able to achieve the goal that you set for yourself, or more.*

*Graduating with a degree that is going to allow you to be happy in your life.*

*I wouldn't really define success in terms of GPA because I have learned a lot while I've been here, but my GPA did not show it. I guess it's retaining things that you learned in class and being able to apply them to real life situations.*

*The definition of academic success is being able to maintain some discipline and strive to do your best and accept*

2

that sometimes even your best is not going to get you the grades you want and to not give up.

Success is being able to complete however many years you have to and graduate. It doesn't have to be graduating with honors—just graduating with at least a 2.5.

I think the main ingredient is to satisfy yourself. If you are happy with your grades, regardless of what they are, if it is the best that you can do, then I think that you are successful.

Academic success would be applying yourself to the highest capacity. Also, having an open mind and open to new experiences. You have to be willing to learn.

I think it is putting in as much effort as you possibly have. Not everybody is a genius or a 4.0. I have never been a 4.0. I don't think I ever will be. But I dedicate my time—as much as I possibly can—and my effort—as much as I possibly can—to pulling my GPA to as high as it is comfortable for me.

Success for me would be utilizing my resources, finishing out the process, and taking that as an accomplishment.

Points to Ponder . . .

1. Do you agree with the students' definitions of academic success? Describe in what ways you would agree or disagree with any of these students' definitions.

2. Write your own definition of academic success.

3

3. Has your definition of academic success changed over the years? Would you expect it to continue to change as you progress through the college experience? If so, how and why?

4. Choose one quote that you particularly like and elaborate on that student's opinion about success using yourself as an example.

_____

## Introduction

Studies show that students who enter college with certain precollege characteristics are more likely to be successful—to make a successful transition from the precollege environment and continue to accomplish the academic and social integration necessary to persist and to graduate.  Among the precollege characteristics that give students an advantage is a history of strong secondary school achievement and academic aptitude.

One reason for selecting the students who participated in this study was precisely **because** their academic records did not meet the standard for regular admission at their respective institutions.  By all standard predictions, they **should** have dropped out of college, as many of their classmates had—including those with strong academic records, as well as those without.  What made the difference for these students?

In the following descriptions, students articulate an acute awareness of the disadvantages and handicaps they faced because of their inadequate performances or poor backgrounds in high school.  It was this awareness, as well as an early understanding of the differences between high school and college, that enabled them to make necessary changes in behavior, whether that meant eliminating their involvement in extra-curricular activities (good and bad) or applying more effort. The common element appears to have been their recognition, even an acceptance, of their handicaps and a recognition of the differences

5

between the two educational experiences, along with a conscious decision to work with it, through it, and beyond it.

Speaking of Which . . .

*I didn't like who I was in high school. When you are in high school, you are kind of trapped in who you are. You have expectations to be that class-clown all of the time, to be that kid who never came to class—and that was me. And the only way that I could get away from that was to start over again. Nobody here knew me. Nobody here knew what I had done, and so from the start I decided to present myself in a different manner.*

*In high school, my father said, "You are not going to college. If you are going to be like this, you are not going to make it in college." And he was right. He didn't know how right he was. I thought he was crazy, but it was true. Fortunately, I had the chance, and I did it.*

*I didn't think of high school as having a real big effect because I was young and didn't realize the importance of an education. Within a year or two, I realized it. Whenever I filled out my application to come to college and saw that there was a chance that I might not get accepted, I got really scared, because I wanted to go to college really bad. That fear kind of told me that I needed to get serious about studies.*

*High school is different from college. In college everybody is trying to find out who they are. In high school,* you pretty much know who you are. You have friends and those are your friends and you basically do what they do. In college you are making a whole new group of friends, and with me, making friends was not the hard part, and being myself was not a problem. But studying was a problem. I had a newfound freedom. I could go out when I wanted to, stay up as long as I wanted to, and come in when I wanted to. And it was like, "Wait a minute!" After the first month, I was tired. I mean, you had school to go to still. You need to be in bed by a certain time so you can get up and go to class. So it was different. For most people, it's what gets you in college—it either makes you or breaks you.

In high school, everything was more social, you know. You really didn't pay much attention to your grades. I mean, that was just the way I was. In college it seems different because everyone is more mature and out of that social thing—which I kind of got out of.

I really didn't do well in high school. I did average work in high school, and I knew that when I got to college it was going to be a different story. I would have to turn it around. And ever since the first day I came, I have just been working hard.

I didn't do anything in high school. Now I learned that I have to do a lot of work myself. So that was the big difference—working, instead of just trying to get through.

I didn't do well the first two semesters, and I was worried about that. Then, it was kind of like high school. I did the same thing. I just kind of got involved in the wrong things.

*High school was like blow-off time. You would find ways to get by in high school. Here it is a struggle. I have to do a lot of work, and I have to do more work in order to just get a C.*

*I didn't learn as much as I should have in high school. I feel like I am still behind in a lot of things and that I am still playing catch-up. It is very tough. It's like, "Oh, my god. This is a constant struggle, because high school was so lackadaisical."*

*In high school, I don't feel that I learned as much as I should have because I was just blowing off classes, so you would constantly use excuses. Here, it's like; they don't want to hear your excuses.*

Points to Ponder . . .

1. Can you identify with any of the descriptions offered by these students? Describe how you can identify with any of the high school experiences and perceptions expressed here. Be specific.

2. What high school experiences do you believe have helped you in college?

3. What high school experiences do you believe have been a handicap to success in college?

4. Perhaps you were not as "lackadaisical" about your high school performance as some of these students describe, but it should be obvious to you that there are some significant differences between high school and college. Recognizing these differences early and making an early adjustment to them can mean the

difference between success and failure.  Describe the differences you have discovered between high school and college.  Discuss the ways in which you have made changes to adjust to the differences. Describe specific behaviors.

5. List three specific behavioral chances you still plan to implement to improve your chances for success.  Also, talk about your deadline for accomplishing your goals.

Goal Commitment and
The Influence of Family                    Chapter 3

---

## Introduction

In the next several chapters, you will learn about the factor that students described as having the most significant influence on their success. That factor is **commitment**. Most often they referred to their commitment as "goals." But they also described commitment in terms of desires, determination, and priorities. Put simply, commitment boiled down to the **intention to succeed**—the **intention** to be successful in the college, the **intention** to get a college education, the **intention** to earn a degree.

For these students, the theme of goal commitment provided the framework for everything else that proved influential in their success. Commitment was a central theme in all measures of success—their achievements, their persistence, and their attainment of a degree. Commitment served to determine their behaviors, shape their attitudes, and guide their opinions. Indeed, it is goal commitment that explains why it was that each of these students—despite problems, doubts, or academic difficulties—was determined not to drop out of college. However inspired, this initial and continuing modification of a commitment to the goals of education was what determined their decisions to persist.

When it came to inspiring that important element of commitment, students described another important and significant contribution to success—the influence of their families.  The following excerpts from their interviews describe a deeply felt debt to family members.

Speaking of Which . . .

I think one major contributing factor to my success is my family.  They were very supportive.  Although my grandmother passed early in my career here, she really influenced me a lot when she was alive—that you need to get a degree, you need to get an education, you need to go beyond just high school, and you need to become something.  All my life I wanted to do something that would make my family proud.

I feel my parents had a lot to do with it, with my values. I knew what I had to do, and I knew that they were behind me. You know, they wanted me to succeed too.  So, they were there for support also.

I know that my parents sacrificed, looking back.  I just want to do it for myself—I mean, just seeing what they went through.  My brother too.  He calls me up to see how I am doing and says, "Just try.  Try your best.  Give it all, you know.  If you give it all you got and you don't succeed, at least you know that you have tried."

I definitely feel like I've been influenced by my family. My parents work hard and they are really dedicated and they are both really hard workers.  They always made me work, you know, work in high school.  My mother has always been really responsible, organized, and has always made sure that I get things done.  I always tell her when I have a paper coming up, and she always asks, "How is that assignment or paper coming?"

My mom was always proud of me and she taught me a long, long time ago—probably because my parents are divorced—to go to school, to get an education, to do what you want with your life, not to depend on anyone else.  I somehow always knew that I was going to college.  My parents never talked about it.  I just kind of knew I should go to college.

My family has always been loving and supportive, and they have definitely, definitely played a big role in my academic success.  Whenever I have been failing, they have been there to pick me up.  If I got an A, they have been there to celebrate.

My parents pat me on the back a lot.  And sometimes I feel as though I am pressured to get another pat on the back.  I don't want to disappoint them even though I know that they aren't going to be disappointed by it.  You know, they support me and they really try not to pressure me.  Sometimes I turn it into pressure.

My sister is one who acts like, you know, "You've got to do this, you've got to do that."  But it's always in a good way.  She makes sure she is looking out for me.  It has helped.

I think that my whole family, in a different way, kept me focused, kept me motivated, kept me encouraged about getting a degree.

I always like to learn things, I guess to impress my dad. I didn't try to get high grades to impress my dad.  I did it for me.  But there is always in the back of my mind, "My dad is *going to be really happy, you know, that I got this." I couldn't wait to tell him.*

*I don't think I had to go to college to become successful. It is nice because it is a credential. But I was living out my family's dream, and once I started getting into it and getting involved, it became a dream of my own.*

Points to Ponder . . .

1. Describe family members who have given you support while you are in college and explain how their help has been beneficial to you in adjusting or succeeding.

2. Describe how your goals have been shaped by the influences of significant people in your life.

## Goal Commitment and
## the Influence of Role Models                    Chapter 4

---

## Introduction

In addition to finding inspiration for their educational goals from the support of family members, students were also influenced to succeed by those they regarded as role models. Most often their role models emerged from the family circle. Students described pressures they placed on themselves to live up to the examples set by other members of the family. Siblings who had been successful in college provided an incentive to several of the students. Parents who had achieved some level of success, either through education or otherwise, were an inspiration to others. Members of the family who had overcome odds or had modeled a strong work ethic were also influential.

## Speaking of Which . . .

*A lot had to do with my sister. At the time I came here, she was in graduate school, and I got to see the ceremony and everything while I was still a freshman. It was very impressive to see my sister come out with a master's degree with a 4.0, and me, an undergrad and thinking, "Look, I could either make it—be right here next to her—or I can fail and who knows what is going to happen." So, my success had a lot to do with the people around me, I think—where I am from, and from my parents, and my determination to be different.*

My father went to a very good college. My grandfather was a Ph.D. from Columbia. Matter of fact, all my family in my dad's family had Ph.D.'s from prestigious colleges. It would be really odd for me not to be in college, and I think I was kind of concerned about being left out.

A lot had to do with my great great aunt who is 97 years old. She had a lot to do with my education; she had everything to do with my education. Grace said, "Well, you will be in college, don't worry." She was a teacher. She just kept telling me, "This is what you have to do. You'll understand some day."

I had an older sister that went here for two years, and I think maybe she has a lot to do with it because she was successful. And then she graduated, and she found a job. So, I think that kind of gave me more incentive, saying, "This is really what I need to do." So, I think she acted more as a role model for me.

It seems that most of my brothers and sisters—they have the same goals. It is just a family thing.

My brother—he graduated from college. My sister did too. And I got a chance to go to college. But they influenced me as I was growing up—helped me get myself together.

My little sister—she was in the hospital for bipolar disorder and when she got out of the hospital and started high school, I have never seen somebody so gung ho to go back to school than her. With my older sister, she has two kids, and she is still going to college. She is a single parent, and one time she worked two jobs and went to school.  If she can do it, I can do it.

My aunt—she went to pharmacy school and became a pharmacist, which is a pretty good thing.  And, my uncle—he went to art school, and one day he just finally said he quit his job and he started his own company—his own production company and he makes toys and board games.  They are both pretty big.

I feel a little pressure.  Not pressure from my family but because everyone seems to have some sort of professional situation.  Before they left our country, my mother was a pharmacist.  My father is a medical doctor; my sister has a masters in social work.  My brother teaches.

I've worked for a long time, and that came from my brother and sister.  They began working at an early age, so as I was growing up, I saw them working.  I wanted to be the same way.  So, at a young age, I started out with babysitting and went from there.

I am going to be the first male that I know to graduate from college in my family.  So, I was raised in the house by three women.  I have a mom, a ma, and me.  My mom was a baby who had a baby.  She moved to another state.  My grandmother had a tremendous amount of hardships and broken relationships.  And I have an aunt that I call Ma.  My mother is head x-ray technician at a hospital.  My grandmother is a legal secretary.  My aunt is independently employed.  She owns a cleaning service.  But I always had to be the man that they never had.  Those ladies, they carried a lot of baggage and it has been my *job to fill the needs that other people did not. So I am fulfilling their dreams.*

Points to Ponder . . .

1. Define "role model." What is the difference between a role model and a mentor?

2. Choose someone whom you would consider to be your role model. You may choose more than one person. Your role model may be someone from your family or not. Your role model may even be someone who does not know you. Describe why you believe this person to be a good role model for you.

3. Have you ever told your role model about your feelings? What are the advantages of sharing your impressions of them and their influences on you? Are their any disadvantages?

4. Find someone you would like to imitate. Why would you like to be like this person? What is it this person does that you would like to do? What benefits would you receive from engaging in the same activities or career this person does? How important would these benefits be to your general happiness and well being?

Goal Commitment and
Being a Role Model                                    Chapter 5

---

## Introduction

Several students described one factor influential to their success
that was a variation on the theme of role modeling.  Besides being
influenced by others whom they considered to be role models for
their own goals and aspirations, many students perceived themselves
to be acting as role models for others: younger family members, older
siblings, other members of their minority groups, sorority sisters or
fraternity brothers, future students, or youth in general.  This
perceived or self-imposed responsibility as a role model served a
beneficial purpose by keeping students committed to their goals to be
successful, lest they set a bad example or otherwise disappoint those
who looked to them for inspiration and motivation of their own.  This
perception helped students to strengthen their own intentions to
persist, and this expectation, whether real or imagined, served as a
constant reminder that their college decisions and performances had
implications well beyond themselves, thereby helping them to keep
their goals and aspirations in the forefront.

Speaking of Which . . .

*My nephew, I mean, like, he is 9, and he knows I am going
to be a teacher.  There are times when he says, "I want to be
like you." His parents are not fluent in English.  I am there to*

look after him to make sure that he does his schoolwork and remind him that he has to do it for himself.

I put in my high school yearbook that I want to be a positive role model to the youth of tomorrow. I still feel the same.

I have nieces and I have little sisters who look up to me. I have godchildren who look up to me and even older people who look up to me, because I am doing something that they didn't have an opportunity to do. They are depending on me to graduate. It is like—okay, I am living for me, but I am also helping other people live their dreams through me.

My brother is 4 years older than me and he just started college this year. So now he looks up to me for inspiration.

I also motivate my family—mostly my younger sisters who looked up to me and even my older sister who is in high school— she just stopped going to school after the prom. She thought it was over, but it wasn't. She lost those credits that she needed, and she had to come back to high school. She had to write a paper in her English class about who motivated her to come back to school and who was her inspiration. She wrote about me. I was just shocked. "Wow! My big sister looks up to me!"

I do drink—and most students do—but I don't drink in excess. I don't do drugs or anything like that. And the way I carry myself, the other African American students automatically consider me as a role model. I know if I don't act right, they will be like, "Well, she did it." I can't tell them, "Do as I say and not as I do." I have to show them what I do. And basically, I take them underneath my wing.

I think knowing that I am going to act as a role model one day helped me also. I know being a teacher, my students—children—are going to look up to me, and I know elementary teachers are extremely important a far as role models. I know that I have to be a positive role model, and that is maybe one of my reasons that I strive to do my best because I am going to need all the skills and knowledge that I can acquire to help my students.

I came back my sophomore year and pulled my grades up, did better. Spring came and my classes started falling down again. I said, "This is a roller coaster ride! I can't do it. How can I keep my grades up?" That is when I started really getting into study skills and time management. And I think it was more or less my little sister. She was like—"If you're not there, why should I go?" You know, she wants to be a doctor. And I found out that my little godbrother wants to be a doctor, so I'm like, "Wow, this is great! Everyone wants to be a doctor, so I've got to keep doing what I'm doing to motivate them to do what they want to do.

I am the president of the sorority now. I was supposed to have study hours when I pledged, but I never went. I would go back and sleep. I changed that around. I make them go to the library. Usually it is from 6:00 to 8:00 they study, and they do not do anything related to the sorority. That is their set time to pull their academics up because that is their number one priority, and I was not having happen to them what happened to me. Seeing them study also gives me drive. Like when I speak at meetings, they listened.

Points to Ponder . . .

1. How does your behavior have an affect on the behavior of others?

2. Do you feel any obligation to do well because others view you as their role model?

3. Are there any members of your family or friends who look up to you?

4. Do you hold any leadership positions that would automatically cast you in the role of as a role model?

5. Is it possible that you are a role model to someone and don't know it? Explain

6. Think about the reasons that you chose someone else as a role model? Do you have any qualities to be admired by someone else? Do you have opportunities that others would like to have?

7. If you knew you were a role model to someone, would that affect how you behaved? Would it affect your performance? Your attitudes? Your language? Explain.

8. Why are role models important figures? How can being a role model help you to identify and define your goals?

## Goal Commitment and
## Early Interests                    Chapter 6

---

## Introduction

When talking about the influences on their college success, several students mentioned the fact that their decision to go to college, or to chose a career that required a college education, was made at a very early age—for some because of an influential experience or family tie; for others because, as one student explained it, "I think I have always had that goal from when I was a kid." With respect to being committed to a goal, these students talked about knowing from an early age what they wanted to do with their lives.

## Speaking of Which . . .

*I always wanted to be a teacher. As early as I can remember, I have always wanted to teach. My babysitter was in college when I was around three or four, and I can remember she used to take me there, and we would go to the museum, the library. I thought the library was just fabulous. Once she became a teacher, she would take me to her classroom. I had a chance to work with children at a very early age. Plus, I had a few teachers during my elementary years that are very influential on me. I wanted to be a teacher, and it stuck. I never changed my mind.*

Well, I just like science. It is just what I wanted to do since I was a little kid. And now I am doing it. It was like—now or never. I couldn't resist it. It is hard to describe when you get a feeling that you can't resist. It is almost like you are not yourself for a brief moment in time.

I used to live in a town with my grandmother, and she owns her own day care. Her day care was with part of the government, so ever since I was with her; I wanted to teach children. You know how kids do—they change what they want to be. They want to be Superman, Batman, ballerina, superstar. For me, teacher was always in there somewhere. I want to be a superstar, but I want to be a teacher on the side. I want to be a ballerina, but I want to be a teacher on the side. Ever since I was young, I wanted to be a teacher.

My grandfather was a lawyer in my country. He wanted my father to be a lawyer, but he didn't want to be one. My father wanted to become a doctor, so he became a doctor. Ever since I was little, I knew I always wanted to be something like, you know, a doctor or whatever. But, I knew I didn't want to be what my father was because—I don't know—something in me just didn't want to be that. When I got to college, I knew that law was where I was going to go because most of the time, most of my free reading and things like that always involved the law or something like that. I read a lot. I mean, when court TV came out that was—gees—that was great for me. I mean, it is boring now, but I have always been infatuated with law for some reason. I don't know what it is. Um, maybe it is genetic. That's what my mother used to tell me.

I don't see how things are set up, but somebody has a plan for me. I like to be the best at whatever I do, and I know *if I would have turned to the bad, I would have been the best at that, you know. But I've always known I am going to do good things.*

Points to Ponder . . .

1. Think about what interested you when you were very young. Is there some activity that you engaged in that gave you pleasure? When you think about doing that activity again, how does it make you feel?

2. Think about someone whom you admired when you were very young. Why did you admire about that person? What kinds of things did you do with that person?

3. Do you recall any early experiences that impressed you? That you still recall as being pleasurable or exciting? What were you doing? Who were you doing it with?

4. What has been your favorite subject in school? Your favorite pastime? Your favorite topic of interest?

5. What would you like to do if there were no restrictions on the possibilities? What is it about this activity or career that appeals to you? What are the rewards you would get from doing this thing? Are there other jobs, careers, or activities from which you could receive the same pleasures or rewards?

6. Are there members of the family or close circle of contacts that you would like to imitate? Why would you like to imitate them?

7. Are you doing something now that you would rather not be doing, but that someone else wants you to do? If you could do what you want instead, what would that be?

8. When was the last time you really trusted yourself to know what you liked or disliked? Perhaps it was when you were eight or nine. Perhaps it was before you entered junior high school when what others thought of you became more important than what you thought. Put yourself back to a time when you explored your interests without hesitation. What did you really enjoy doing? How can those interests be translated into a goal or a future career?

Goal Commitment Inspired by
Unusual Circumstances                                   Chapter 7

---

## Introduction

It makes no difference from where a commitment emerges.  Two
students described some unusual events in their background that had
a strong impact on their educational goals and commitments.  They
shared interesting and moving stories about how their goals had
developed.  One student described his tortured existence in school as
a child because of a facial abnormality that made him self-conscious
and the source of teasing, making it difficult for him to apply himself.
It was not until he was twelve years old, when he entered a children's
hospital for the first of a series of operations and came into contact
with children who had terminal illnesses such as cancer and leukemia,
that he began to feel grateful, actually "lucky," and resolved to make
the most of his life and every opportunity that it offered.

A second student, a nontraditional student close to the age of 40 who
had earned a G.E.D., explained his decision to go to college as the work
of "divine intervention."  He described a scene that occurred in the
shower, where something hit him so hard that he went down on his
knees, and, thinking he was having a nervous breakdown, asked God for
help. The result was an "overwhelming push" to quit his job and do
whatever it would take to go to school, because, as he explained,
"There was no choice in the matter. The choice was no longer mine."

In each of these cases, the genesis of the life's goal—in one case, to
make the most of everything, including an education; in the other case,

to go to school no matter what— was accompanied by the power of strong emotions. And in each case the commitment (the "change," as the older student called it), preceded the college experience, paving the way, as in the case of those influenced by prior family influences, for the likelihood of a successful outcome.

Speaking of Which . . .

The student with the birth defect described the process as follows:

*I was born with a cleft lip and palate. So when I was young, it really had, I thought, a negative influence on my life, because, grammar school—elementary school—was really hard for me and I was really a horrible student. I didn't pay attention in class. I had a lot of problems in class because I didn't look that good. I had like a major underbite at the time, and my face was kind of distorted, and a lot of the students made fun of me and, you know—for about seven years. So, then I was diagnosed as having a learning disability. So, I was in this program. They really couldn't pinpoint it. I think it was more— looking back now—it was more emotional. I had more emotional problems than learning problems because once I was in the program, the classes—the classes were a lot smaller for one thing. So, it was a lot easier for me to concentrate. I got a lot more one-on-one attention. I wasn't distracted as easily as I was in the bigger classes. And I found that I could do the work.*

*So, I went from being like a D student to like a B-plus, A-minus student. It took me a couple of years. It took me awhile,*

28

but by high school I was back to where I should be.  But I had to make up a lot of ground because I feel I really lost a lot in those really important years, like 1st grade to 5th grade.  I had to overcome what I lost, and I struggled for a couple years to make up what I lost— reading, writing, arithmetic.  I've been in and out of hospitals for surgery.  I mean, I realize that it could have been a lot worse.   What really influenced my life was seeing young kids not only with the problems I had, but kids with cancer and leukemia who really weren't going to see their 15th birthday.  I think that really influenced my life—seeing that.  If those kids were me—in my shoes—they would make the best out of every day that they had and go on to do something extraordinary because they really understood how important life was and how precious it is.  So, I kind of looked at it like that.  I said to myself, "You know, you are really lucky.  What you have really isn't that bad.  It is totally correctable through surgery.  Now it's kind of a nuisance, but in the long run it will all be corrected.  So, you should make the most of your life, and everyday you should try to, you know, focus in on what you want to do.   Just try not to take things for granted and make the most of my opportunities because a lot of people don't have the kind of opportunities to, like, get an education like I have, or the health.  You know there are a lot of kids who have really bad health problems who can't go on and, you know, do what they probably would do.   Or it is a lot harder for them to do that.  I went to Children's Hospital when I was around eleven or twelve years old.  I always asked myself, "Why me? Why did this happen to me?" But then I saw how bad it really could have been—you know.

The older, nontraditional student explained his reason for quitting a job and enrolling in school as the work of  "divine intervention."

*I'm telling you, I started feeling real, like crazy. And I thought I was having a nervous breakdown. I got down on my knees in the shower one morning and said, "Okay God, what is the problem here? I am going nuts! What is the problem?" And the next day I got up and picked up the phone and told my dad I was quitting my job, moving out of the house I had, and I wanted to move home. He thought I had lost my mind. And here I am. It happened. I had no idea I would even do it. That was just an overwhelming push to do that. It is weird. You can't describe it, but it was what I was supposed to do. So, I gave three months notice—well actually I got another part-time job first, and I got accepted here and gave a notice to my employer, who didn't believe I was leaving. He gave me $2.00 more an hour to stay. I still left. There was no choice in the matter. The choice was no longer mine. I know it's an odd story. The choice is no longer mine. The choice is out of my hands. My dad thought I was really nuts. He said, "I'll be right there." He came up to be sure I wasn't drinking or something worse.*

Points to Ponder . . .

1. Not everyone has had the kind of emotional experiences that these students described, but everyone can think of something that has touched them deeply, in either a negative or positive way. Can you recall such an incident? Do you have a circumstance that you believe has shaped your choices? What are the positive outcomes that you can make from such circumstances or events?

2. The first student describes himself as being grateful for what he

has and of using that gratitude to make the most of his opportunities.  Try using the following exercise to improve your attitude: Keep a list of 5 items each day in your journal for which you are grateful.  Be as detailed or general as you wish, starting each sentence with, "I am grateful that _____."  The idea is to develop the habit of seeing the value and opportunities available to you no matter what and of focusing on the positive aspects of life rather than the negative.  Either focus is a matter of habit.  To develop a positive habit, keep your list for a full month.  See what difference it makes in your day to day view of things and of yourself.

3.  Are there any activities that you engage in where you feel that something outside yourself is driving your behavior?  Many people describe creative endeavors like painting or playing music as having that effect.  The same can be true of anything that deeply captures our attention and interest, that makes time stand still or pass without our realizing it.  What can you learn about yourself and your interests by recalling such moments?

Goal Commitment and the
Negative Behavior of Peers                    Chapter 8

---

## Introduction

Successful students described how by observing the self-destructive
behaviors and failures of other students, they were influenced to
refine and reinforce their own educational commitments. Once in the
college experience, these students were able to secure their resolve
to be successful and to keep their focus on their goals by observing
the negative behaviors of those around them and watching the results
of those failures and bad habits.

Negative behaviors were described by the students as those that
detracted from an academic focus (for example, missing class, wasting
time and money, acting "uncivilized," using drugs and alcohol, partying
excessively). Although they knew it was important to be adequately
integrated into both the social and academic circles of college, they
also knew (or had learned) that too much emphasis on social activities
at the expense of the academic ones could lead to disaster. As a
result, they were able not only to avoid such behavior when it
detracted from their academic goals, but also to actually make use of
what they observed as negative behaviors in others to strengthen
their own positive ones. As one student put it, "I use other people's
weaknesses to fill my strengths."

## Speaking of Which . . .

*I can't be here and be wild. And plus, when I came here I met people who truly redefined my definition of wild. There was no way I could hang with what they were doing. Maybe I was intimidated by my own negative aspects. I thought I was pretty good at being wild. There were people who were better at it. I let them be the ones.*

*I think it was their attitude. They looked at things completely different than I did. Where I was from, I looked at things as the only way to keep what I had was to have an education.*

*There are your friends who are in college. Then there are your friends who have done nothing. And it is kind of embarrassing to go back and see your friends who have done nothing, and you can see it on their faces—that look. I think I was worried about falling into that category.*

*I learned a lot from other students, too. It is unfortunate to take someone's failures and say that is a benefit to me, but I think that happened. I really looked at a lot of people and I said, "You know what? I don't think what you are doing is really going to work. So I am going to sit back and watch you and if it works for you then maybe I'll take it up. But if it doesn't, then maybe I need to stay away from it." And those people are not with us any longer.*

I have had friends who are positive friends, ones who are negative friends. Most of the guys at the fraternity—they are positive in the fun life, but when it comes to school work, their habits and how they go about their goals—it's mediocre. You can follow them and pick up their habits, or you can, your know, be an individual and have your own habits. I mean, they are your friends, but that does not mean that you have to pick up their habits. You have to analyze your friends and see how they are as an individual and how they are as a student—what you want to pick up and what you don't want to pick up. I mean, if your friends can't respect that aspect, then they are not your friends.

I knew where and when to party—when was not a good time. I had a lot of friends who I realized were not thinking on a college level. That is not who I wanted to be, so I said, "Let me sit back and watch these people, see what happens to them. Right now, I have been told that I need to be in the books, so that's where I'll be. I'm just going to watch."

People who sit in class and do nothing, those who turn in assignments late, who don't come to class, people like that—that's not what I want to do.

This is one thing that I have seen. I am the type of person that—this is just one example—whenever I am in a classroom, I am sitting there and listening to the professor. I am there for a reason, and I sit there and act civilized. When I am on campus, I act civilized. There were a lot of students on campus my freshman year, they acted like they were never out before.

*Some students are just wasting money that I wish I had. And it really upsets me and I know other students who feel the same way.*

*I don't want to fall into the gutter.  I know too many people that are in that situation.  They are somewhere they really don't want to be.  They made a mistake in the past that they can't get out of.  I just don't want to do it.*

*Some people—they get here and their eyes are all wide. Upperclassmen tend to drag on the freshmen.  I mean, that is how it all starts—those first couple of weeks.  I've seen a lot of people fall after the first couple weeks are up.*

*I was there once in awhile, you know.  I worked with a lot of guys that went to jail.  They were crazy like I was, and they used to get into trouble all the time.  Now I try to tell them there is another way.*

Points to Ponder . . .

1. Try doing the following activity for a week: Pick a class that you are taking.  Observe the behaviors of the other students.  Make a list of all the behaviors that you see as undermining or hindering success in that course.  Then compare your own behaviors with those you have listed.  Are there any that you need to change?

2. Do the same exercise with behaviors you see outside the classroom.

3. Do you have difficulty saying "no" to your friends or to others you would like to have as friends? If so, try using the following statements: a) I prefer not to _____, or b) I don't feel comfortable _____. Make a list of examples from your own experiences, where you need to respond quickly and want to say no. Then explain how you could do so by completing the response statements for each example you cite.

4. Do you have trouble listening to your instincts, or even knowing what they are when it comes to making decisions? Try using the practice the students describe here of using caution when you are in a new situation or don't know what to expect. You can always change your mind later when your better judgment prevails.

5. Studies show that the first few weeks of college can be crucial in a student's decisions about persisting. Certainly, the freshman year is crucial for establishing a strong beginning versus earning a poor record from which you may never recover.

   Based on your experiences so far, what behaviors are you engaging in that should help you achieve a strong beginning? What behaviors are you engaging in that may threaten your changes of early success?

   Complete this exercise by then setting some goals for changing the negative behaviors you have identified. Be specific about the new behavior you will substitute for the negative or absent one (for example, "I will attend every class session"). Then establish a deadline for completing your goal and sate the expected outcome (for example, "I will begin this new behavior immediately and will have a 98% success rate"). Finally, monitor your progress with your goal on a regular basis (say, weekly) and assess the outcome at the end of your final deadline.

## Goals as a Means to an End                    Chapter 9

___

## Introduction

Finally, with regard to developing and nurturing a goal to graduate from college, several of the successful students described their commitment in terms of a strong desire to achieve something they really wanted, to secure a future career, or to get their money's worth out of the college experience. For these students, it was not only helpful to be motivated by family expectations or the desire for personal and intellectual development, but it was also important to them to see their goal as a means to an end.

Speaking of Which . . .

> *I think the biggest factor is the attitude that I know that I had to go to college in order to get a good job. I put my mind to it that this is what I was going to do, and I was going to finish, and you know, get a degree.*

> *I looked at things as the only way to keep what I had was to have an education. And, where I come from, I am used to seeing people have a lot. And the only way I could keep that and maybe do better was to have an education.*

> *I would not feel comfortable in places that I would want to be at, if I did not have a degree, which is not to say if you*

have a degree, you are a genius. But it is just a sense of security I think some people feel.

I think if you plan when you are young—not exactly what you want to do, but have some kind of idea of what you want to do, what you would like to do, what you are good at—then you will end up with something you also love to do. I'm going to do what I want, and I want to be a psychologist.

This is the only way to succeed unless you are an athlete of some kind. You can't really do anything without going to college. I want to make money and do well in life. You can't just sit around and I'm not the type to go into the service or anything like that.

I think knowing that I have to pay for my education has a lot to do with my success because in high school, I really wasn't caring about my education as I am in college—knowing that I need an education to get a job, knowing that I will hopefully be successful after I graduate—those are the keys.

That is what I am paying to go to school for—to do my work and get my grades and get my degree—to get out of here and find a job.

I want to go to as many job fairs as I can—just hand out résumés. I am going to find something. I am 22 right now. Hopefully, I will find the first step to the overall goal. Just be happy—that is my goal.

Eventually I want to go on to get my masters and Ph.D. But first, I just want to be proud that I have a degree. My goal *is to graduate and try to find a decent job, just so I can get my feet wet, so I can have some experience.*

*I just knew I needed to go to college because I just thought, "Well, what am I going to do with my life after high school?" I want to have a job. I want to make money. I want to build a house." Those are my goals.*

*There are so many things that I want to do with my life that if I don't get an education and if I don't do well and make myself known, then I am never going to be able to do the things that I want to do. I want to travel. I know that I need to perform here and then get my foot in the door at a good company, work hard there and move up until I can make a name for myself.*

*I didn't have any choice but to have a divine sense of accomplishment. A lot of people—they dream and that is all the dream is—a figment of their imaginations. My dreams are not a figment of my imagination. My dreams are ultimately the plan of what I am going to have tomorrow. That just kind of intensifies my desire to accomplish higher things. It is not that I want to have a whole bunch of money—but I know that I will.*

Points to Ponder . . .

1. Although a formal education is no guarantee for success, having a degree can serve to reduce the limits on your freedom. For example, studies show that workers who have a college degree have a higher earning power over time than those who do not. Also, college graduates are more competitive in the job market and more

able to change jobs when they wish. Describe your career goals for the future. How important will it be for you to have a formal education in order to accomplish those goals?

2. How do you plan to prepare for your career while you are finishing college? What kinds of extra curricular activities will improve your skills in your career area? What additional educational opportunities can you engage in that will improve your chances of getting the job you want later? What other benefits can be gained from engaging in additional activities, such as an internship, a work-study job on campus, a peer-helping role, or a leadership position? Research what kinds of opportunities are available to you on your campus that will help improve your chances of securing the kind of job you want after college?

3. What are your dreams? How can you turn your dreams into a plan for the future? How will having a dream help you to develop day to day goals as well as long term goals?

## Making a Transition, Developing, and Maturing
Chapter 10

---

## Introduction

At this final stage in their college experience as successful students and graduating seniors, students were quite able to reflect on the progress they had made in their personal and academic growth and development.  They were conscious of the importance of having made a the necessary adjustments along the way—of having made successful transitions, particularly early in their college careers.  These early periods of adjustment appear to have been crucial to their success.  When students identified a time period in their description of a transition or critical period of change, they tended to talk about events, circumstances, or conditions in their freshman or sophomore years.

## Speaking of Which . . .

*I think it was more of a personal-type development that happened very quickly.  I came from high school, where I was not the model student at all.  They say that when you come to college and you are away from your parents it frees you.  Well, I think mine did the opposite.  I got to school, didn't have my parents to watch me, and I did better.  It was not that they were holding me back in high school, but it was time, I guess, to* prove to the world that I can do something by myself. I was just becoming more mature.

I think the biggest adjustment period is during your freshman year, because if you don't get off on the right foot, it is all downhill from there. You end up being here for years. Even though I didn't do as well as I wanted to during my first semester, coming back in the spring the spring, I decided it was either make it or break it for me.

I have been able to interact with administrators on campus—able to network with people and talk to people. With the activities I was in on campus, like student government and a lot of the things that I have learned in class, I can use in other types of situations and just in general—talking to parents or whatever. I seem to have grown through that, and I have been able to use those skills that I have learned for class too.

My confidence has grown so much. My freshman and sophomore years, I was so unsure of myself. I would always sit in the back of the room. I never wanted to be in the front. Now, I am always in the front of the room, and I'm always talking to people. It is so easy for me to interact, and a lot of times, I have to make comments to the whole class and I am the one the whole class counts on. That is a very big stepping stone, you know, because some adults can't do that.

I wasn't so confident before. There is so much that happens when you are in school. It is 4 years, and each year you are growing. You are learning new things. A lot of things get easier as the years go on because you are used to the classes, you know what to expect, and then a lot of things get harder. You get used to handling situations. You get used to life. It is hard, but you are never sure what life is going to bring and you learn how to deal with situations.

I would react to different situations and then look back and say, "That wasn't right." Not that I was making a spectacle or anything—it was just that I was at college, and people weren't acting like they were in high school. That was one of the major problems that I had. But I realized it on my own. I saw what I was doing, and it was time to stop to grow up.

A critical period would have been my freshman-sophomore years. It was the first time I was in a situation where people aren't from the same small town that I was from, and they didn't have the same beliefs. Everyone was just different. I was never in situations like this before.

I think I learned how to be more open-minded with people, because when I first got here, I didn't really like anybody. More often than not, I didn't give them a chance. I am learning how to do that now. That is a positive thing I think you have to do. I have definitely gotten better with that and have developed that habit pretty well.

I know there are a lot of students like myself. When I came in as a freshman, I was naïve. I didn't really know anything about it, so of course, you are going to go out, and you are going to party. You are going to come home at 2:00 in the morning, and you might have a test the next day and try to cram in two hours and try to study. Believe me, I have done it. I have learned through experience. It really hit me whenever I was put on academic probation my sophomore year. Then I had to realize, "I am going to be thrown out of school, then, what am I going to do? What academic success did I achieve in being thrown out of school?" Obviously, I wasn't accomplishing my goals, because I wasn't applying myself.

I came down hard on myself. Looking back on that, it was like, "What was the big deal?" But that is another part of development, of developing even though you aren't realizing how serious you have to be. You have to find out that you have to be somewhere between serious and realistic.

You just have to move patiently. Patience is the expression of your sophomore year. You just have to go step by step. You just can't advance extremely fast.

I remember changes—things like writing more effective papers. It seems like every year, since my freshman year, I have gone home for the summer, and each year my papers have developed better and better. There is nothing I consciously did, you know, but, as I read, I see that my vocabulary grew and things sounded a lot better. And I compared a few from senior year with the first and second semester of my freshman year, and I was like, "You know, there is a big difference here. A lot of things have changed." But still, if I read scholarly journals, I can see a difference between my work and their work. So, I realize that just because I graduate from college, it's not going to be easy. There is a still a lot of development—a lot of growth.

I think we all have a reckoning point. I just realized, you know, my life is going nowhere. I went through a world of wars, lost a job, I was totally drunk for about two years and then—I didn't want to live like that anymore. I just changed—who I hung out with, what I did—everything. If you're a troublemaker like I was—I was a criminal, a juvenile delinquent-- you have to *change first. I started living a different lifestyle. I still wouldn't have been here if I hadn't had that awakening thing. When I was 30, I just changed my whole life.*

Points to Ponder . . .

1. Have you noticed signs of maturity in yourself since you have become a college student? What are some specific ways in which you have changed and become more mature, more separated from dependency on your parents, perhaps, and more able to make your own decisions?

2. Have you made any adjustments in your behaviors with respect to your academics since you first arrived to college? What have you changed?

3. What about changes in your attitudes? What specifically is different about you? What would you still like to change?

4. What about your level of confidence? Have you been able to see any improvements so far? How have these changes been manifested in your behaviors?

## Having, Nurturing and Retaining the Goal

**Chapter 11**

---

## Introduction

As students made the appropriate adjustments to college life and college classes, their goals became even clearer and their commitment to succeed was further strengthened.  Making successful transitions, developing personally and academically, and moving steadily toward greater maturity went hand in hand with the process of having, nurturing, and retaining their goal commitment and their intentions to graduate.

Speaking of Which . . .

*When you start to become a junior and a senior you have to start thinking that your goal is half accomplished.  My goal was almost there, so why should I work harder if I am halfway to what I want?  So, at that time, I had to think of another goal.  I had to almost reprioritize and say, "Okay, look, this goal is almost accomplished, because in two years I am going to have a degree and that is coming quicker than I think.  So, what do I need to do after that?  Do I need to think about where I am going to work?  Why am I going to do that?  Where am I going to be happy?"  These are questions I was asking myself at the time.  I was just kind of floating along and saying, "Look, this is easy.  I have got the hang of everything.  I know how to write* these papers in an hour. I can take a test. What is going to go wrong? Everything is fine." The only reason that I think that I failed is that my priorities of the future were not in sync. I was like, "Well, I will graduate, no problem." You have to keep that fire strong of reaching your goal and then when you see yourself reaching that goal you have to make another goal. That is what I didn't do until I got that letter of dismissal. Then I said, "Okay, now I understand, and this is why I needed this letter." I knew I needed to graduate, but I didn't know why. What is this going to do for me? I think my behavior was not setting goals after I had seen myself reaching it. I have grown up to realize that I always need to have goals.

I just try to set realistic goals for myself and I always try to do my best on a test. Like always, I want to get an A, but I try to get a B. And if I get an A, that's great! I just try not to have too high of expectations, you know, reasonable expectations that I know I can definitely achieve.

In high school I enjoyed my history classes and it was probably some of the only reading that I did, you know. But when I did it, I enjoyed it a lot. So, I started thinking, "It would be nice to teach history." At that point I was thinking about being a high school history teacher. Then as I got to college and I saw how history professors are in college, I was like, "Ah, this is a lot more enjoyable for me. This is something I like a lot more—their job as opposed to the high school half-babysitter, half-teacher." And I'm like, "I think I'm going to shoot for that. I might get better." So, ever since I did my history major that is what I strove for.

You have to deal with so much. I mean, you have to deal with people that you live with. You have to deal with budgeting your time.  You have to deal with possible financial problems.  Just getting through those four to five years and graduating—that is the goal.

Sometimes I'm like, "I can't do this anymore.  I give up.  I quit."  Then something always pops in the back of my mind, "No, you can't quit—not quite yet.  You still have a little more energy left.  Keep going."

When I first came to college I was all gung ho.  I thought, "Okay.  Study.  Read.  Study.  Read.  All day long."  That is what you were supposed to do when you are a freshman.  Everybody has that anxiety.  You don't know what to expect your first day.  I had to learn to relax.  That is a big thing for me.  I used to stress out over tests.  I used to have really bad anxiety over things.  I would be paranoid right away, you know, freak out.  But then after awhile I started to realize I have to graduate.  I'm not going to be at McDonald's flipping burgers the rest of my life for $4.25 or $5.25 an hour.  I have to want to achieve the maximum goal that I set for myself.  My goal is I want to graduate with a degree, eventually you know, move on for master's, eventually move on for my Ph.D., and I want to go out and help people within the community.

I finally, after searching through myself, I found this desire that I _wanted_ to graduate, I _wanted_ to make myself proud and make myself feel that I have accomplished this on my own.  I wanted my parents to say, "You know, my daughter did so well in college.  She made it through.  She graduated."  Same thing with professors.  I want my professors to think, by participating in class, "She knows what she is talking about.  I feel comfortable giving her this grade in this class.  She has the desire to get an A."

*My first goal was to get into this college. I mean, I tried so hard. I accomplished that goal, and my second goal was to go through not being on academic probation or anything like that, but having average grades, trying as hard as I could, and finally getting my B.A. or B.S.—whatever I was going for. And, I achieved the first goal, but the second goal—I didn't see it in sight. I was a sister in my sorority, and I could easily go out every night and party and throw academics off again. But for some reason, I had this desire in me that—after I cried about probation and after I saw how upset my parents were and my advisor —I realized I had to do this for myself. I had to turn this around.*

Points to Ponder . . .

1.  As these students learned, having a goal to graduate is not enough. One has to have both short-term goals **and** long-term goals in order to keep inspired and motivated. In addition, it is important to think about your goals, to dwell on them, to find ways to keep them in the forefront of your mind and your imagination.

    Write a set of both long-term goals and short-term goals. Within each list, order the goals according to the time it may take you to accomplish them. For example, at the top of your list of long-term goals might be your intention to graduate from college. Under that you may establish a goal of graduating within a certain time period. You may add that you intend to complete an internship or a cooperative education program in your senior year. Perhaps you can work in a study abroad program during your junior year. You may have a goal of adding another major, or transferring to another major. In order to compose your list, you will have to do some research on what is available, what steps you need to take to accomplish them, and what time frame is required to work them into your plan. Doing the research and the planning, considering your options and the advantages and disadvantages of each, all these activities help to engage you in the process of creating your goals and also having an investment in seeing them accomplished.

The same applies to your list of short-term goals. Pick a time period, say the semester, to start your list. You may decide, for example, that your top goal for the term is to make a certain grade point average. Then you will want to decide what grade you would want to achieve in each of your courses in order to accomplish that goal. Next you could establish the goals for achieving those grades. Set gradations to your list until you are able to create short-term goals for the week, or even day to day goals. Write them down. Cross them out as you accomplish them. Give yourself the reward of seeing the results of having followed through with your intentions.

2. Check to see that the items on your lists of goals are realistic. You do not want to underestimate your abilities and compromise your dreams, nor do you want to set a goal that you have no chance of accomplishing. Again, you may have to do some research if you are to understand what is involved in accomplishing a particular goal.

3. You may have noticed that the students whose descriptions you are reading had developed a habit of talking to themselves—of engaging in self-talk. What have you noticed about the quality of that self-talk? What do you do when you experience a slump or

when you just don't feel you can continue on the path you have set for yourself?  Do you engage in positive self-talk?  Do you talk to a friend or relative?  What works for you?  Share your secrets with your classmates.

Decisions about Involvement                    Chapter 12

---

## Introduction

Becoming involved in extra-curricular activities can be an important factor in feeling a part of the social and academic systems of a college or university.  These activities can help students develop both the skills and interests that support their educational goals while, at the same time, help them to establish a sense of belonging.

Although several of the students did become involved in institutional activities, some students believed that they needed to limit their involvement in non-academic aspects of the institution, believing that such activities took the focus off their main goal and threatened their ability to accomplish it.  For these students, this meant limiting the many extra-curricular activities they may have wanted to participate in, at least until they were able to establish a strong footing in the academic arena.

Other students described many examples of positive involvement in college activities, involvement that was both rewarding and helpful in developing skills and strengthening their goals of academic achievement and success.

Speaking of Which . . .

I did a lot of things here. Not as much as I would love to do. Like I would have loved to be a part of so many organizations, but I just didn't have the grades or the time.

I wasn't really involved in anything extra. I look at people that are playing sports, and I wonder how they ever have the time. I mean, there are people that succeed, but I don't know if I could do that or not. I feel like I have so much time taken up in my classes.

I was walking on for baseball try-outs. I made it through those. I was on the team basically for the fall. We used to have to do this workout all the time. We had to do this regimen which just kills you, three times a week or four times. I was too tired. I didn't care at that point. So I took the summer to get myself together and start over. I figured the only reason to be in baseball or football, especially in a university like this, is if you are going to go on to the pros or whatever. And maybe, if you are on the football team, you have that idea. But most don't go anywhere. So there is no point. It was fun. But when it ruins my schoolwork, then I can't do it.

I had offers to join fraternities and that stuff, but I would rather not. I mean, my social life was fine when I got here, and it's still fine. And another thing was time constraints. I just couldn't budget time for them. I had more important things to do. Nothing against organizations like that. I think they can be fine. If I had more time, I would have maybe participated in more of that stuff.

I pledged. I went through the whole thing. And that is why my GPA got so low, I think. I was just thinking about how I overcame not letting the social life bring me down. Once you look at what you want and what those organizations want, sometimes they are not the same thing and you have to choose one over the other. So that is what I had to do. But a lot of the social things, like student government—that is a social function that was contributing to my future also. So you just have to weigh things.

Student government, extracurricular activities, being elected class president this year—that was such an accomplishment. There is so much that has come out of that that I never dreamed. My senior year—I think I have accomplished more this year than I have the whole three years. There is so much—being connected to the administration, connected to student organizations, being on the student senate. That has all influenced me a lot.

My freshman year, another student was the president of student senate, and he encouraged me to go out for it. So that was really neat. So I said, "Okay, I'll run." And then we did a little campaigning outside the student building and it was really nice. And as years went on, we kept doing it.

When I was in high school, I always tried to excel. It is not grades all the time. I was class president. I was on student council, enviromental clubs, Shakespeare troop. I played tennis. In college, I am in the nationality club. I was president and vice president of my fraternity and I am president of an honor's fraternity.

Sometimes you'll work yourself to death to the point where you don't feel like studying anymore. So now I'm in a lot of different organizations—student union, student activities board, a sorority, gospel choir. I go to the movies or something.

*Being in activities keeps me going and also helps me to prioritize my time and everything. I still have to keep a minimum of 2.5 to stay in my major and to hold an office in an organization. Rarely am I not busy.*

*I was in the accounting club—vice president—the investment club, tutored, intramural sports, government and work-study. It seems like the more you talk to people, the farther you will go. That is the way I always thought about it. You become smarter and more knowledgeable talking to people. I think those activities enabled me to do that.*

*I am on the selection committee for incoming faculty. You know, I get to see the president. I get to talk to him. I am a student advisor, and I am also involved in other organizations.*

Points to Ponder . . .

1. What activities or extra-curricular involvements can help you to stay focused on your purpose for being in college. Explain.

2. Some activities that are available to you may undermine your purpose for being in college and others may enhance it. Based on your personal assessment, make a list of both kinds and explain briefly why you believe each is a hindrance to success or an enhancement.

3. How can staying busy help you with your time management efforts? Have you been able to determine what is "too busy" for

you and what is enough to keep you challenged and motivated without overwhelming you?  Explain.

4. Studies have shown that having a work-study position on campus can lead to greater success with classwork.  Can you explain why this may be true?

Considerations about Leaving College
Dropping or Out                                    Chapter 13

---

## Introduction

Quite interesting were the students' responses when asked if they had ever considered dropping out of college.  For a group of students for whom this decision should have been a constant threat, given their predicted chances for success, the answer to this question for most was an emphatic "No, never."  The majority of responses to this direct question could be summarized by one student who said, "I never even considered it."

That does not mean that these students did not struggle with threats to their academic standing or doubts about being enrolled in the right college.  Several students considered transferring to another institution.  One student talked about a brief period, during the summer following his freshman year, when he considered postponing his education.  Another was forced during that first summer to consider dropping out because she had been placed on academic probation.  But only 1 of the 16 participants actually dropped out of school, and only then with the expressed intention of returning—which he ultimately did, transferring to another institution at the same time.  One of the students who found himself academically dismissed at the end of the freshman year simply refused to accept this condition.  He campaigned to convince his dean of his commitment to succeed, proved it by successfully completing summer school, and consequently received permission to return his sophomore year.

Again, as in issues concerning transition and adjustment, it is interesting to note that the major struggles with decisions regarding persistence or withdrawal, even transfer, presented themselves to these students during the very early stages of their college experience, specifically during the freshman year or shortly thereafter. It would appear that for these successful students, the commitment to complete an education overshadowed any serious notion of abandoning their goals. The following excerpts are examples of the students' position on the topic.

Speaking of Which . . .

*The thought never crossed my mind. I don't know why because I actually did get a nice dismissal letter—but it was not until that time. And even when I got a letter saying, "You are dismissed from the university," it did not affect me. I said, "No, I'm not."*

*I had a lot of stress on me. I was still a little guilty from when my grandmother died. I was like, "It was all my fault. I should have been there. She wanted me to be there." And then there were a lot of other things. I really didn't want to be here anymore. I wanted to be done. I wanted to get out of here. So my grades started slipping. I started taking heavier loads, which wasn't good. Classes I didn't like, I would just stop going to. And it was like, "That is not why I am here. I need to really sit down and think about what I want to do." So through the summer, I thought about all of the things I wanted. And for me to do that, to be successful, it was like, "Wow, I need to get out of here, but I need to pass these classes. I need to get* reinstated." I was just going down the list of things that I needed to do, and I did them all.

In between my sophomore and junior years, like I had bills galore and I was talking to my dad about it. My bills were minimal to what a lot of adults have out of school. I got a very good summer job, and I was thinking about leaving school then. It was the best job I have ever had in my life. It was paying my bills. All my bills were paid. And then all of the sudden a few weeks before school started, I started getting bills again. My car went out and a bunch of different things, and it was just stressing me out. My dad talked me out of it. It wasn't a really hard decision. It was just an option I was thinking about.

I didn't consider leaving school, but I did consider transferring to a different college. It was more because I didn't feel like I was getting the college experience. I am a commuter, and I just thought, "I will try this thing on campus for a semester." But I don't live far from here, so I found myself at home everyday. And it is so expensive to stay here, and to me it was really a waste of money. And that was the only reason that I considered transferring. But, because I feel I'm at a good university and I am getting a good education, I stayed.

Yes, my freshmen year, second semester, I wanted to take a year off. I'm like, "Hey, I got the freshman year under my belt. Maybe I should just take a summer semester and, you know, do some different things." I enjoy canoeing, hiking, backpacking, and I'm planning on going on with my education—taking a year off and then going for my Ph.D., trying it in history or perhaps law school. I had this fear—and I've had this fear since my freshman year—that I am going to get old and I'm not going to be able to go canoeing, backpacking and hiking the way I want to, you know, and climbing—mainly rock climbing. But then I realized—"How many years do you want to take to graduate? Five? Four? Six? Let's get moving, you know. Once you graduate you will have plenty of time, you know." That is another reason why I am taking a year off between grad school—to do all the preparations for that, with applications and tests, stuff like that and to have a little bit of time to relax.

Well, I've had fleeting thoughts. None of those were serious. No, I want to finish. I want to make money. That is the only way to do well in life. You can't sit around. I'm not the type to go into the service or anything like that. I did want to transfer at one point, but that was only for a couple of weeks.

I haven't given up. I haven't quit. I got friends that I talk to and my parents. I have a lot of support from people, including like two advisors that I have on campus—and fellow students.

No, I never really thought about leaving college, not finishing college. No, just switching colleges. It's just, "Well, maybe I need to take a break and go somewhere else." But it was here that I ended up staying. We moved around a lot when I was younger, so after four years, I figured, "Okay. I need to move somewhere else." So, I didn't feel like I was being successful. But then I got talking to people and they were like, "Well, you don't have to move. You can stay put." And, I did and got basically done now. Yeah, there were times—you always get into times where you feel like you're not going anywhere and you are ready to quit—it gets too hard. You basically have to encourage yourself and get encouragement from others.

> Sometimes I'm like, "I can't do this anymore. I give up. I quit." Then something always pops in the back of my mind, "No, you can't quit—not quite yet. You still have a little more energy left. Keep going."

> No, never. I didn't even think about it. No, I knew I had to just stick it out either way. I mean—either way I figured, no matter—after the first year if it got worse or better, either way I would still be here. I knew it would get better anyway because I just can't let it get worse. That wouldn't be me.

> Oh, yeah, I did consider leaving. I wanted to transfer someplace closer to home—to another school.

The only student who actually dropped out at one point explained his reason as follows:

> It was my concern about my parents at home. There weren't any extra finances coming in and I like to maximize their life. You know, I like to give them what they want, pay off their house, etc. But that was the only time that I considered leaving. But I would have came back ultimately. That was the primary objective for me determining to leave at that particular time—was to go and take care of my parents.

But as he had promised himself when he dropped out, this student ultimately returned to college, transferring to another institution in the process. He described the events leading from his decision to drop out of college to finally re-enrolling:

> Yeah, I did stop going to school at one time. I am 24 years old. I will be 25 in July. I went to another university, a

black university in another state. I really didn't know much about financial aid. I just wanted to leave—get away from home. And I went down there for a year. Financially, it killed me. I had a 3.48 GPA, but I had to come back. So, I came back, got an apartment. Matter of fact, I was the co-owner of a duplex. I always had this thing—business inclined. I met a guy and we worked together, and we went co- on a duplex. So, I moved upstairs, and we rented downstairs out. Then I said, "Oh, I got to get myself back in school." My grandmother's house was flooded with people because she is kind of the nucleus of the family. I wasn't going to go there. Too many grown people under the same roof is chaotic. So, I moved out. I got my own place, got into community college. I was driving trucks and working. I bumped a couple of heads and stuff, stopped going to community, started working full time, went back to community, finally finished up at community. And, my brother— he went here. He is not my biological brother, but since he was young, he was in and out of my grandmother's house. So, because I was moving around so much, we really didn't get a chance to spend much time together. So it was his last semester and he was like, "Please, come on, finish."

So, I said, "Okay." I called my grandma and said, "Grandma, I am going to take a run up to the university." She said, "Okay. I'll see you when you get home." At that particular time I was giving her money and stuff, helping to pay for things. I came up here, met an advisor, talked to him, and met an admission officer. He gave me an opportunity, opened a window of opportunity for me to come here. I called them on it and I went home, said, "Hey mom, I'm going back to school!"

Points to Ponder . . .

1. It is common for students to question their decision to be in college or to be at a particular college. There are many reasons for doubt, especially during that first year when there are so many changes and adjustments to be made. You may feel as though the decision was never really yours to make, that you were pressured or expected to attend college. Perhaps you feel lonely or isolated. Perhaps there are problems at home that keep you distracted from your efforts to adjust to your new home. Perhaps college is not what you expected. Whatever your reasons for doubt or discouragement, it can help for you to realize that you are not alone.

   Research the ways by which you might receive help with adjustment issues at your college or university. Make a list of the possibilities: Are there support groups, an advisor, another student, a faculty member, or a family member that you can confide in? Is there a freshman seminar course on your campus that you can enroll in? How about a counseling center, a tutorial center, or an advisement center that you can access? What about a church group, your residence hall advisor, or your roommate as a source of support? Talk to an upper-class student or other students in your classes about your concerns. Consider finding a job on campus or volunteer some hours of service to a campus or community group. Any effort that will help to make you feel connected to the institution and to others will also help you to develop your goals and increase your commitment to remain.

Developmental Program Support and the
Precollege Summer Experience                    Chapter 14

---

## Introduction

Different aspects of a college or university can have either a positive
or negative influence on the decisions of students to persist.  As
these students reflected on the most important contributions to their
success, they described some features of their respective institutions
as influential.  There was one aspect in particular, however, that
received their praise the most.  Every student, without exception,
attributed credit for success to features of the support program or
the developmental education program in which he or she had been
required to participate.  In particular, they emphasized the
contributions of program personnel and the advantages of being part
of precollege summer experience.

Along with having a commitment to succeed, having an initial and
continuing commitment to the particular institution can be a positive
factor in promoting a student's persistence.  Interestingly, none of
the students in this study described a particular affiliation, strong
attachment, or exceptional fit with the college or university from
which they were graduating.  What they did voice, however, was a very
strong affiliation, attachment, and appreciation for their support
programs.  As they reflected on factors in success, each of the
students, without exception, gave credit to the faculty, staff, and
services of his or her developmental program.  They were particularly
appreciative of the opportunity this kind of program had offered
them, in some cases because it was the only key to enrollment in
college, and in all cases, because it had prepared them so well for the

entire college experience.  This was particularly true of their opinion about the precollege summer programs that the majority of these students had been required to attend.

Speaking of Which . . .

*When classes started, and we were in classes with the rest of the students, that was kind of hard.  Then it wasn't, because I knew so many more students that the regular students did.  I met so many over the summer.  So we were walking around campus like we'd been here for a year or two. We knew where everything was.  That was good.  But I really had to adjust that summer.*

*I know that the summer program, to me, helped with my transition.  Just being aware of the campus ahead of time. That helped.  And the way they teach you how to take notes, how to answer multiple choice questions, and how to listen—I didn't know those things until the summer program.*

*I know that I gained so many things from the summer program.  I am sure that it had to influence me a great deal. One of the greatest things is adapting to college—being familiar with the college campus before those other freshmen. I made friends before anybody else had.  And those guidance counselors—my advisors—they have been a great help.*

*Initially, when I entered college, I had no idea what the program was about.  I honestly thought it was just another "quote-unquote" program.  But the program was designed with classes that create an educational foundation for you and assist you during the transition from high school.  I found it very* beneficial because I wasn't as prepared for college as I thought I was. And certain classes—such as study skills, writing class, a math class—just helped me prepare for the rest of the college courses.

When I graduated from high school I had to come to a program here in the summer. It was about a month long, and we took 6 credits, and I know that that helped me a lot. I think if I didn't go to that, I don't think I would have made it because I think that helped me form the commitment. That was a good program. And I did good at that program. I got an A in English and a B in Psychology. It helped. It gave me confidence. That is what it did. And every semester since the fall of my freshmen year my grades have gone up each semester—even if it was just a little bit, they kept going up.

Nobody had explained to me what it was. They said, you know, "You were accepted to college based on your performance and opportunity, and if your performance is not up to par— meaning if you don't get above a 2.0—then you won't be admitted your freshmen year." Well, that of course scared me. I'm like, "Oh, gees! I have to jump right into college courses and do good in them. I can't get any Ds or anything"—which I was so accustomed to getting in high school because I didn't do anything. So, I started doing everything I didn't do in high school, and it worked out and I did well.

They really had a good summer session. I wasn't sure about how it was going to be at first, but it was actually pretty good. It was really, really good. It was five weeks. Probably everyone should do something like that because you get acquainted with the campus, the library, even the little things, like where you eat, where to go for fun, and even stuff like that is good. You learn. It was tough. I tell you. I probably did *more work in that five weeks than what I did the first semester. They had you going like all day and you had night class. You learn interesting stuff and valuable tips. It wasn't too hard; it was just busy. But they really did a good job. I thought it was a really good idea.*

*I think they should require freshmen to take classes during the summer. I think it is to their advantage. You get a feel for college.*

*The program is my family. So you know, coming through this program in '93, at first it was like, "Man, I don't want to be here in the summer." Then I got to meet people the first day here. Everything worked out. Four years later, I'm getting out, and I'm still working with the program. It's like they never leave you. They are like a part of your life because you come in through the program. You work with the individuals. They help you regardless. Even when I was kicked out, you know—on probation—it's like, "We're going to work with you to get you back in. You just sit in the study skills class and learn what you got to learn."*

These students were so convinced that this early experience had made the difference between their success or failure in college, that many wished that all students could have a chance to experience the same advantage. This strongly positive attitude of developmental students toward their program status defies one of the more common myths, which claims that at-risk students feel stigmatized by their participation in developmental programs. At least with respect to these successful students, that generally held impression is far from the truth.

Following are some typical examples of students' descriptions of the value of summer or precollege programs in helping them make a successful transition and build an early foundation, their recommendations that this experience be offered to all freshmen, the recognition that the developmental program gave them an important opportunity, and their acknowledgment that any negative reactions they may have had to program involvement were brief at best.

Speaking of Which . . .

It has been an influence. I mean, my girlfriend now, she is like, "I wish I went through that program. I am sure it would have helped me."

I think all freshmen should have to go through like a six to eight week program like when they get out of high school. I mean, they have all the other summers after that. It kind of helped out. You get a head start going into that August or September. I came here and I just didn't know what to expect. I don't know—I just liked the people when I came here.

This program really helped me because I wouldn't be here otherwise. I wouldn't have gotten accepted to the university with the regular requirements that you have to have to get into the university. So, this program really helped me, and that is number one. They took the time through the whole summer, and I was able to work on what I needed to work on to be able to compete with other students.

I think coming through this program contributed to my success because they gave you an opportunity to try to catch up, you know, to come in the summer and try to get on target with the rest of the kids that came in your freshman year. So, I think that contributed to my success as far as the support—the services offered. So, I think if I didn't come through the program, I would be worse off now than I was. I didn't feel like I was a dodo or a dummy. You know, it was like, they are going to give me an opportunity to work on what I don't know in a way that I can succeed in college. Which I have done.

I really am grateful. If I was not admitted through this program I would not be here. I wouldn't have been admitted at this particular university.

Throughout the years, I saw a difference in my skills and ability. It is really hard to explain sometimes, but I try to explain it to other students—if you are having difficulty, sit down and talk to someone. I always refer them to people that I know because I can give them more advice on how it benefited me. A lot of students will go and some students will not, just because it's like, "It's a program— I'm not in that program." And, it's weird how a lot of students think the same way. If I was not admitted through this program I would not be here. I wouldn't have been admitted.

Every time a new group of people comes through the program, I always talk and tell them, "Look, it's not a bad thing, you know. They are giving you the opportunity to work on skills you don't have or that you are weak in that you want to make stronger. And just use it. Use it to the best of your ability. Even when you are out of the program, always go back." You know, like I'm always here. So, it is very helpful to have these programs in place for students who are lacking in certain areas, to bring them up to speed and make them feel more important in the college atmosphere.

Well, at first when I got the letter, you know, I was a little upset. I am like, "I have to go to school in the summer," you know, "This isn't fair." But I am really glad that I came through the program because coming in as a freshman is a very big transition and just some of the things they helped us out with—like scheduling. That was like a big deal. I know you talk to other people who did not come through the program, and they had no idea, you know, what classes to take or even how to schedule. So, just little things like that really helped me. And also being up here during the summer. There weren't as many people here. You got to know the campus. You got to know the workings and everything. So, when I came up for the fall semester and all these people are around, I don't think it was as big of a shock or as big of an adjustment.

I didn't have a problem with it at all. I knew that I would need help because I do have a slight case—and I didn't realize it until I was in 11th grade—but I do have a small case of dyslexia. So I knew that I would need some help.

I wasn't scared to say that I was in a program. If someone asked me—some people are like, "No, I'm not in that. I don't do it." I am proud to say, you know, that is what really kicked me in the rear for me to straighten myself out. I was not embarrassed to talk about it, and I was not scared to. I mean, if anybody asked me the question I would be very honest and tell them, "Yes, I was in for two semesters." Yes, that is what pulled my grades up and if it wasn't for my program coach I don't think I would be here today. I know I wouldn't be here today. And that is to be honest.

Initially, I felt terrible, because I thought it was just some program. I didn't know what the program was all about. And before I came I didn't research it. It was like, "Oh, I'm admitted through some program. I want to go to school, so I'll go through this program." But once I got here and we were given the information—more about the program, and why we are in it, and what it's supposed to do for us, and what we can do for the program—I thought, "Well, that can't be too bad. Someone here to help you—constantly." It centers on you and it's focused. You are a smaller number of students in the entire university. I thought, "Well, this might work out."

As far as having any problems with it, you know, I guess as a class we looked at ourselves as being special in a sense that when the first day of freshmen year rolled around and everybody is walking around going, "Dah?" We already knew what to do. We were already acclimated into the environment. We already knew what was going to happen. We already know what our first day of class was going to be like. We already had, you know, our schedules already done and everything like that. We knew where all the offices were. So, in that sense we were, you know, we were better. Okay, but at the same time we are like, "Well, why were we here in the first place?" And then we just laughed about that. Then we were like, "Ah, no big deal because we got in. It doesn't matter." That is probably the way we all felt. I knew a couple of other people that felt the same way. Rather than looking at why we were there, we looked at the advantages. We could always find something good. And we are all cool about it, laugh about it, what a pain in the butt it was, you know. We all considered it such a pain in the butt because the dorms were on fire—hot in July—and we were stuck there with a curfew, you know. Ah, man, so, we chuckle about that. And we're still here, and because it was the quickest six weeks ever. We thought it was going to be an eternity. You know, we had never done a course in just 6 weeks: I mean, it was like the whole year in high school.

Hey, this is not a bad program—not at all. I enjoyed it. If I had to do it over, I would come through another program, you know. Because it helped me in my time management, my study skills, going to tutoring, working with groups. And it was fun, you know. You get to meet a lot of nice people that you will not meet in your major. It's like; they could care less about you. You know, you are just a number over there. Here they know your name. It's like Cheers—they know your name. But over there it's like, "Who are you?" Your advisor doesn't know you. You can't even speak to the secretary because she doesn't know you. It's like, "What do you want?" It's like, "Wow." It is so cold. You can speak at least, you know. So, this is like home. You *can hang out here and learn a lot.  Just talking to people you can learn a lot.*

*I didn't want to do it.  I wanted to be accepted in the regular way, like everyone else was accepted.  But then I thought it was kind of neat because—it was preppy.  I didn't like it at first, but when I got here it made me realize what I needed to work on, and it was like a wake-up call because I thought I knew more than, you know, what I did.  But—oh, I really enjoyed the program.  I really enjoyed it.  Just the initial coming here.  I had to come senior week after we graduated from high school.  So, I wasn't looking forward to going back to classes.  I just graduated.  But when I came to the program it was a very, very good program.*

Not all of the students in the study had participated in a summer program. Every one of them, however, had that important early involvement that seemed to connect them to something in their institution that they could depend upon, not only during the early transition period, but also whenever they needed support, encouragement, or assistance.  This kind of general and continuing support was not only utilized and appreciated, but also helped create the connection to the institution that may have been missing through other avenues.

Speaking of Which . . .

*I can say I have felt connected.  I depended on a lot of people in my program.  Maybe not to make my academic success, but maybe to keep my strength and believing in keeping my goals alive.  Sometimes I was saying, "Why do I need to be here?" If it was not for my educational counselor I don't think—I am pretty sure—I know—I would not be the same, because she kept me so focused, so much alive about who I was outside of academics.  Like, "Well, this is what you* need to do," and it is like, "Oh, yeah, you are right." You come away from school, you come away from home and you don't have anyone to tell you right from wrong. You might not need anybody, but you always need somebody to tell you, "Look, stay focused." Somebody from the outside looking in can tell you more than maybe you can tell yourself about the situation you are in. If you are willing to accept that, then you will be successful. If you are not, then whatever happens to you, you kind of asked for it.

As far as the program goes, I have always felt connected in the sense that if I needed help I knew where to go. I knew exactly where to go. Even when I was out of the program, I never considered myself going to my professor as an advisor. I never knew who my advisor was, and I never trusted anyone else. That, I think, was the key. I never trusted them. They told me something—I learned to always back it up.

Most of the older people here right now, I would say—a good percentage of them that started in the program—when things go tremendously wrong, this is the first place they come to, the first person they trusted here. It always comes back to "Who can get me out of this trouble?" Well, I remember the first trouble that I got into, which was that first test that I took. "Who got me out of that? I gotta go there." It is just like—no question, you will always go back. It's a sense of security. There is nothing wrong with that—that is a good thing. In that sense, I have felt connected. As far as anything else on campus, I guess I really wouldn't know because I never wanted to stray, to lend my trust to a lot of other people. Not to say that they are not trustworthy. Just to say, for me, my best interest was in the comfort of here. And that was all I needed.

That program is very helpful. Every time I talk about my college experience, the program always comes up. It's like that was the root of my success, you know. They started to bring me up from the ground. Like, "Okay, you're dirt level right now but you will sprout up to be a success. You are going to be one of the beautiful flowers on graduation." I was like, "Wow! That's great!" Because it is like a big support program that I see. It is like, "Oh, my God, I can go to my advisor. I can talk to the director." Most people cannot talk to the chairperson in their department, you know. I mean, this is a big thing for me. I was like, "Wow. I hope my little sister comes through something like this, you know.

Earlier, like my freshman and sophomore year, I struggled a couple of times with, like, the family life, with people passing away. My counselor has always been there—my program guidance counselor. There are counselors that help you with your courses. I mean, some people enter college without a good guidance counselor or who aren't there for them. Theirs job is more like a friendship. It's more like, when scheduling, you would come and you would just have them sign it. Whereas in the program, they are actually there to look after you and to me that has helped out a lot.

Throughout my four years, the learning skills center has provided lots of support in different ways. The tutorial services are very beneficial, and the staff is very supportive in whatever you do. They may not have all the answers, but they are a resource center, and they will help you find out the professor or the organization or the business company or anything. There are no limits to what they will do for you, and although it's not in their job description, they go far beyond. And that was very beneficial because I had no support anywhere else on this campus. During my four years, there are maybe two professors that I can say I could go to for issues that pertain outside of their classroom. And sometimes it was even hard to find a professor who you can go to with issues that are _within_ their classroom. Whenever I had a problem or was unsure about something, I would go to the learning skills center before I would go to whatever office I was referred to. I would always speak to my academic advisor there. I had another academic advisor in the school of education, but before I went to see her, I always went to see my academic advisor at the learning skills center. He helped me preplan my program for the four years, monitored me carefully, and if they see that you are trying, they are always willing to help you. But even when they see that you are not, they are still willing to help you. And they see you trying, they won't hesitate to do anything for you. If they see you are slacking up, they will give you a call and won't hesitate to stay on your back. It is really nice to know that someone is doing the job—what they are actually supposed to do. I try to refer a lot of students to the learning skills center, and they won't turn you away just because you are not enrolled in their program.

Now I'm not even on campus, but I find myself over at the learning skills center, because it is a resource center. It really is. A lot of people don't know about it, and they are missing out on a lot of resources. I have received tutorial services from the learning skills services. But, I would still refer other students to the staff because they are just so warm and loving and supportive. They are just a big support staff and it's like a family there.

My program counselor would send me mailings saying, "Just checking up to see how your semester went." And there would be a special note, "Please call me at whatever time" or something to that effect. He was very supportive. I don't know if everyone else in the office knew what was going on, but it just seemed like they did because everyone was like, "Are you okay? How are you today? Did you do this work? Well, how did that class go that you were typing up the paper for? What did you get on the paper?" They are always checking up on you. They want feedback. When they see you again— and it could be two months later—they will ask me what did I get on this paper that they helped me work on. It's like, "You really remember!" It gives you a feeling that someone else really cares about you receiving an appropriate education. Not like some students who can be advised to take all the wrong courses or the advisor allows them to choose courses which are not appropriate for their program. Then they fall behind.

The people are like a support team. If they don't have the resource there, give them a little bit of time and they will point you in the direction to find out where the information is or they may have retrieved the information for you. So, it is very helpful, very beneficial. I am glad that I was admitted through this program. I am very, very appreciative to the people there. We had a banquet or an appreciation dinner for our graduating seniors, and I had to speak there and I let them know. It brought tears to my eyes. I told them, "You just don't understand. I really appreciate what you've done for me over the four years."

You know when somebody cares about what they are doing. You know when somebody is just doing a job and you are just a piece of paper. And, that means everything to have someone that is supportive and willing to go the extra mile for you and all that stuff. That is more important than anything.

I had a really good advisor. She was excellent. I felt like I had a weak advisor my freshmen year here, so I didn't really get to know him. He was chair of the department, so he was so busy. I never got to see him. When he did see me, all he did was sign my card, and it didn't matter what classes I signed up for. She actually showed me that she cared, that she wanted me to do well. She was my backbone the whole way through. I was on probation that semester and I pulled my grades up. I mean, taken from spring of my freshmen year, my GPA overall was like a 1.2. So, I was pretty deep. I was able to pull it up to like a 1.8 my sophomore year, and they said, you know, "Go another semester on academic probation, go into the program again." So, right away she started harping on me about, "You know, you got to do this, you got to do that." And then I pulled my GPA up. That semester I think I got three A's and a B. So, I did fairly well, and I was able to pull my GPA up to over a 2.0, which took me off academic probation.

When I was in the program, I had an advisor. I never heard her put me down. She only gave me positive things, and I think that is what I needed. She sat down with me; she went through my classes. If I needed help with a paper, she was always there to go through it. She also told me my sources that were available, and I also knew that I could go to her for, you know, questions. I would always go through my schedule with her first. I would always go through like all my papers with her. If I had a test she would quiz me or make up a test for me. All I had to do was let her know what the material was on. She was very supportive, and she was always understanding. They know me there. I'm not just another social security number, not just another student number in their file. And, I think that is what a lot of other advisors and professors need to do more on campus.

My advisors in the program really showed me the way. They sat down and said, "Listen here. This is how you want it to be. You are going to have to accomplish this. This is what you have to achieve. This is how much you have to pull your GPA up." You know, they were always there to show me resources and show me the way. I think that was what their whole role was.

They are a good program. There is always advising available, one advisor you usually go see. My advisor is still my friend now. It was nice. He had a little office, and you could always stop in. I am in there every day. I just stop in all the time because it is a nice little atmosphere. Everyone is very nice. It is a nice little place to go.

The first thing you do is you write your academic work plan and you lay out your courses you have that semester and your goal GPA and what you want to get in each course, and they will say, "Well, that is your goal GPA." So then, midway through the semester you come in and you say what you have in each course. If it is below when you chart it, then you see what you need to do to get it higher. You can get some tutors, or if you know what you need to do that helps, then you can do it yourself. I mean, after awhile I learned how to do it myself. "Oh, here is my GPA, and I can figure out what I am doing." But you know, some people need that. And I needed that at first, and then I got myself on the ball, and then I didn't need it real quick. It was like, I didn't need my parent for a little bit.

That is one office here that is friendly. They personalize this university for a lot of people, which is good.

Well, here in this program you don't say that they are deficient. You say that they are different. Speaking to difference, I will put anybody in this program against the best students out there because what I find that—you know, say that if we were to go into a depression right now. You would get kids jumping off the Honors College killing themselves, you know, jumping out of the highest floor. But the program students would be just fine. They will continue to succeed, and ultimately they will be the leaders of society. I have a problem, especially when we start talking about the funding that places like this get, you know. Where does our money need to go? We need to facilitate human growth versus some nonsense just to make somebody else look good.

I talk to everybody here, and I try to draw something from everyone's experience. I can talk to them especially about my emotional needs, you know. They remind me of my parents. I don't go to them for pacification, but I go to them for truth, you know. I talk to the people that grabbed me as soon as I got here—those are my parental figures. I know that they have my best interest at heart. They have demonstrated that, you know. Whether I need financial help or whatever, they have been there for me. So, I have a certain *level of trust, and I know that they don't like me—they love me. Even now, my advisor—we get along great. I mean, you know, sometimes he will say something sharp to me, but it is okay. I mean, that is what dads do. It is something that I needed. My father was never there.*

It is safe to assume that this commitment to the developmental program, one which had lasted in many respects throughout their entire college experience, had become for these students not simply an adequate substitute for institutional commitment but, in essence, a better one. In many ways it made up for any of the negative institutional aspects the students may have encountered. If they were not embraced by their department or by individual faculty members, they knew they were embraced by their program. If they found no help from the institution, they found it from their program. And if they were not particularly proud of, connected, or committed to their institution, they remained so in some fashion to their program, throughout their college career. And for those students who attended a large institution, their program participation was the key connection that helped them find the necessary niche to make a large institution seem small.

Points to Ponder . . .

For student participants in developmental education programs, summer programs, freshmen year seminars, or other college support programs, answer the following questions:

1. If you were speaking to new students entering your same program, what would you tell them about the benefits you received from being a part of such a program?

2. As an upperclass student who has learned from both your mistakes and your best decisions, what advice would you have to share with new students to get them started on the right foot?

3. Describe the ways in which your participation in a program of support has prepared you for college and helped you make adjustments from high school to college.

4. How have your study habits changed compared to high school? What specific study strategies have you learned as a result of your participation in the courses or activities of your program?

5. Do you make use of all the resources that are available through your support program or through other agencies and services on campus? What else could you be doing that you are not?

6. Did you have a negative reaction to the requirement or expectation that you be part of a support program? Did that attitude change for you? What caused you to change your attitude?

7. The students in this study describe an appreciation for the opportunity to participate in a support program. They also describe a strong appreciation for the services they received and the people who helped them. Would you agree with their perspective? What does this acceptance say about the maturity level of these students and about their commitment to themselves? Do you believe you have achieved the same level of maturity and commitment?

8. What specific benefits did you discover that you received when you compared yourself to other freshmen? How did this make you feel?

9. What would you say to other students about your participation in such a program? Would you promote the services to others?

For students who have not been enrolled in a developmental education program, a precollege summer program, a freshmen seminar course, or other support program, answer the following:

1. Perhaps your campus does not have a formal course for new students or a precollege summer program. Perhaps you did not qualify for a program that helps new students make adjustments to college. Nevertheless, it is important for most students to find someplace they can go for support or to identify people who can help them with developmental issues. Using whatever sources you can, locate all the resources of support available on your campus. Investigate the details of one such resource and present the information to your classmates. Be sure to include details such as location, phone number, contact person, mission or services, and procedures for utilization of the resource.

2. Is there a learning resource center on your campus? Is there a tutorial center? Is there a central advisement center? Are there courses that can teach you the skills and knowledge you need to function effectively in your institution? Have you used any of the services of such centers? If not, why not?

3. Do you have a place to go where you feel comfortable, a place where you are not "just another social security number?" How can you make significant connections with caring people on your campus? Who might these different sources of help and concern be?

4. What organizations or efforts can you become involved in that will support your academic goals and also contribute to your personal

development?  In what specific ways will such organizations or activities benefit you?

## The Importance of Faculty Support    Chapter 15

---

## Introduction

Any form of faculty support, wherever and whenever it could be found, was valued as an important contribution to success for students and a valued form of affiliation.

## Speaking of Which . . .

*I have found more relationships with faculty members than I have with students. They know me. I go to their house to eat. I just get a tremendous amount of support from the faculty here on campus.*

*There are those professors who come off that they are caring. They want you to succeed. It makes the class a lot easier, and it is not as fearful for you to go ask for help because they show you that they care and that you can come and they will help you. The professor can have a lot to do with your success.*

*When I am struggling, I go see the professor right away. I don't waste time in that aspect. I go see them.*

*If I make a connection with a professor then I will make it a point to go talk to him a few times throughout the year and* just chat—chat about the class, chat about a paper I wrote for them. You know, see if I can get anymore information about the class. I have no problem about going to talk to professors.

My favorite professor is in the English department. He has helped me out and I have no problem going back and seeing him.

My experience with the faculty is great. There are always a couple of bad apples in every barrel. There have been one or two faculty members that I haven't particularly cared for. But the vast majority do a heck of a good job here. You can go to their offices. They will sit down, and they will help you. I you have a problem, you can go see them and you can work things out.

Especially here, because it's small—you can go see faculty when you have problems. A lot of them will talk to you about your daily life problems besides school, which is good. I mean they are more your friends than your teachers.

There is one teacher in the education department who has helped me a lot. He helps me with papers for other classes. He won't do it for me, but he will help me. For me, faculty have been a big help whether it is re-reading my papers, helping me with punctuation. Faculty are important because they can make or break you too. If they like you, they will help you.

A big choice for me was going abroad, because then I really got to know the professors who came with us. I got to know them all. I am going back in the summer to visit one professor. I really got a more personal experience. Then, when I came back, I started to get to know more people because I *was in higher level courses immediately. So I got to know a lot more of my professors.*

*He is one of the professors who got to know me. Out of three big lecture halls, he got to know me. I could just go in and I could talk to him. When I was worried, I would go in and talk to him. "What if I never find a job? What am I going to do?" "You will find a job." He always had confidence in me that I would do well, that I would get a 4.0 and that I could keep it.*

Points to Ponder . . .

1. Students can benefit greatly from interaction with faculty and from faculty support. Faculty members make good mentors and can help students develop career interests. Describe how a particular faculty member has been able to help your development, inspire your interest in learning, or encourage you to pursue a particular career.

2. Do you seek out the help and support of your professors? If not, why not? Make a decision to improve your access to this important resource that is yours for the taking. You have a responsibility to yourself to take advantage of the availability of faculty as a resource and service as well as a source of knowledge and wisdom. Make a decision to improve this aspect of your college experience. What are some things that you can do to avail yourself of the knowledge and wisdom of your professors and receive their attention and interest in you as a serious student?

The Importance of Peer Support                    Chapter 16

---

## Introduction

In addition to faculty support, students also talked about the importance of support from their peers. Here, they described two types of support—emotional support from friends and academic support from fellow classmates.

Speaking of Which . . .

> For projects or assignments—if you are not quite sure of things that are needed, you can ask other people. You can have study partners. First of all, just talking, getting to know people. Then you kind of figure out who is the right person for you to be studying with. Just talking and then saying, "Hey. Do you want to get together? I really don't understand this. Let's meet at the library sometime." And then you can meet and go over notes or study for the test or something like that.

> Another important thing is support from other people. Especially, I would say, getting to know people in your classes because they can have a lot to do with it. You can rely on them.

> Friends are very important too. I have one best friend who comes up and helps me all the time. She has a car. She takes me to interviews and stuff.

*In some situations you turn a lot more to your classmates. When they all come together and say, "He's not going to help us," or "She's not going to help us. Let's figure this out ourselves."*

*A couple of people in my classes that I have known through the four years here, like I can call them, and we can go work on something together or help each other.*

*If I have a problem in a class, if I have an assignment, but it doesn't seem to be working out for me, I might start trying to solve my problem by going to a student that I know is a little bit more proficient in the class.*

*I know you are supposed to go to your advisor and everything to schedule classes, but I think you should go to students also.*

*I have always been fortunate to have good friends for the past four years. I have learned a lot from them, and I think they've learned a lot from me.*

*With philosophy and the one class I took in religion—that was my toughest semester. I had to get help from people who were doing well in the class.*

*I have about five or six really good friends, and we always talk about stuff. It is good to have someone to talk to that is not in your family, about stuff like school and whatever else is going on. We have a pretty open relationship.*

My sorority sisters, we have known each other since we got here. And when I have a problem I go to them. Whether it is something personal or academics, I can go to them.

My friends basically help me to calm down. They are stress relievers. If I want to scream, "Alright, let's go scream." If we need to talk, we sit and talk. They are there for me.

My friends have been very supportive. Those who do not attend college are excited about the things that I tell them. They are proud of me and happy for me. I haven't gotten any negative vibes from my friends.

I pretty much have made this big university a smaller place myself. I met people in my dorm. We hang out together, we go to the movies, and we go to dinner. We do all kinds of things together.

Another big thing for success, especially at this university, is that if you are not into the Greek thing, not into the sororities and fraternities, you have to make your own group of friends. You have to find your own little niche where you fit in.

Points to Ponder . . .

1. Describe how the support and influence of your friends have contributed to achievement, effort, or success for you.

2. Do you belong to any organizations through which you have met friends who can support your purpose for being in college? What are these organizations and what are the ways in which your academic efforts are supported and encouraged through these friendships?

3. Do you have one or more friends in whom you can confide? Discuss how having such support helps you.

4. Are you a good friend to others? Reaching out to help others can have a reciprocal effect. Explain why.

5. Successful students learn to use whatever resources are available to help them to achieve their goals. This includes making use of the skills and knowledge of other students. What are some ways that you can think of to do likewise.

6. Are their any forms of structured peer support at your college or university such as from tutoring centers, advising centers, social clubs, or academic clubs? List the various places where such support can be found. Find out what is involved in accessing these services. Make a decision to try them out. Develop a plan that works one or more of these services into your academic plan. Start now.

7. Teaching others is the best way to learn something yourself. Collaborative learning, learning that occurs between two or more people, can be a powerful way not only to learn the material at hand, but also to learn "how to learn." Does your college or university provide such collaborative learning opportunities, such as through supplemental instruction, group learning, homework helpers, or workshops? If not, how can you take the initiative to create collaborative learning situations?

8. Do you seek out the help and advice of other members of your class? How can you go about getting their help, especially if you are struggling with the course?

9. Have you considered applying or volunteering for positions where you are the helper? Studies show that not only is peer support one of the most effective ways for students to learn, but the person providing the support receives as much if not more benefit from the experience as the person being helped. Can you explain how and why?

## Roadblocks to Success                    Chapter 17

---

## Introduction

When asked about roadblocks to success, some students focused on personal and financial problems or described work commitments that challenged their academic goals. For some, these problems emerged when they were asked to discuss a time in their college experience that they would describe as a crucial period.

Not unlike other students, this group of students had to cope with events and circumstances that were not in their control. Untimely deaths of family members, illnesses (their own and other's), and variety of personal problems arose to distract them from their academic focus.

Unlike other students, however, these events and circumstances challenged the already tenuous hold many of these students held on their likelihood for success. One more problem to solve, one more hurdle to clear, one more thing to think about could all prove overwhelming. As one student described it, "You end up struggling the whole way through."

In addition, the majority of these students, unlike some of their peers, were compelled to deal with financial issues. Most had the demands of one or two jobs to juggle along with their academic challenges, while others had to consider the burden of carrying financial-aid loans into the future, whether they were successful or not.

## Speaking of Which . . .

*You wind up struggling the whole way through. It was okay to do it your freshman year, but every other year it was the same—like my grandmother's death, and then family calling me with every single problem in the world— like I can control that? But, I shouldn't have allowed all those negative influences to influence my academics. But yet there is nothing that you can do. Your parents need to let go. You've got your own stuff to deal with, you know. I don't want to deal with their problems. I have my own. I think just allowing your family to know how you feel and tell them, "Look. Back off. I am trying to do my best here and you're not helping." They have to understand that you don't always have time to sit and talk, and write, or come home.*

*I have so much going on. I am the manager of an off-campus dormitory. It is privately owned, and it is a 24-7 kind of job. I am a live-in manager. So, I don't have to pay to live there, but I don't get paid. I don't get a paycheck. But I got lucky—really lucky. It is a big help. I have been there for a year and 9 months—the whole time since my parents moved away, I have been there.*

*I recently lost my grandma and a lot of other things were going on. I've worked. Throughout my four years I have worked two part-time jobs and I went to school full-time every year. So, eventually it just starts to take its toll and along with that and other things, school was becoming last. Fortunately I didn't fail any courses or have to withdraw. A lot of times the* counselor, my advisor, would call me and see if I was okay or send messages through people that he knew would see me and say, "Well, get in touch with him. He wants to see you."

Tragedy happened in my family when I graduated from high school. My brother died, so I didn't want to leave my mom and my sister, so I just stayed here. He passed away a few months before I graduated and I had already had all the different acceptance letters, so I wasn't sure where I was going yet. Once that happened I decided that I would just stay near home since I applied here, just in case—so I would be at a school in a city. And it was a good thing that I did because I don't regret staying here at all.

I didn't know how expensive the school was. I didn't know how I was going to pay for school because at first my information was incomplete on financial aid reports. We kept filling them out. My mom and I kept doing it wrong. She never had done this before as far as financial aid. We were putting in the wrong information and not getting the appropriate information from my dad. They are separated. It worked out, and I received some late funding. And it was like, "Next year, what am I going to do?" So, I applied sooner, and they said, "You have to apply for loans also." And it was like, "Oh, no! I didn't want to do that. How am I going to pay the loans back?" I thought about it, and I thought about it because at first I was going to transfer just for that reason alone—to a less expensive university. I didn't want to have to pay back all this money once I am finally done. But, then I just said, "Oh well. If I have to pay back forever I'll just pay." And so I stayed.

*The only thing that affected me applying myself has been working. It takes a lot of time out of my day, and going all day—nonstop most of the time—is pretty hard. I try to fit studying in between, but sometimes I find my study time being sleep time. I work in the evenings—and when I get home I'm tired. I'm preparing for the next day, and I may not complete all of my assignments. So, I'm up early in the morning trying to complete them before I leave. But to work was my choice. Initially I didn't have to. My mom didn't want me to. I wanted to. And then I moved out on my own so then I had to. So, I changed from what I wanted to do to what I had to do. I've gotten used to it, but I'm also tired, really tired.*

*At the end of my freshmen year I got mono, like most freshmen do. And with the mono I was going to have to miss class. And as a result of missing class I got really scared, because I didn't miss class like that, you know. I have always made it to every class unless I slept through one or two here and there. But, I never just skipped. And I was going to miss class, and I got anxiety over it. And the anxiety just kept building and building. I had it all that summer, and, you know, there is still traces of it. I had to take a week or two off and just lay in bed. It was like a week and a half, and because I missed those classes I'm like, "You know, I'm going to miss work and finals are in two weeks and how am I going to be able to pass finals?" And, "Are all my professors going to understand?" You know the ones that I had talked to said, "Yes." The ones that I hadn't had a chance to talk to got a letter, but who knows if they are going to understand. It is the end of my first year and I might totally blow it because I got sick.*

*A critical time for me was one year when my dad got sick and was in the hospital. I missed a couple weeks of school, and then I got sick and missed another couple weeks of school.  It was a dismal time.  The turning point is that it got better.  That was a make or break kind of time.  I didn't get the grades that I normally do that semester.  It was things that I couldn't handle.  I would say that was the turning point, though.  No matter what, I am going to finish.  That was the resolve.*

*I worked up until last year.  Well, I never had any free time.  So, eventually what I did—it was only part time anyway and I wanted less and less days and then they wanted me to go full time—so we parted company basically.  I just couldn't give them enough time.*

*I only have one job this semester, but usually I have two.  With two jobs, I worked in the minority affairs office and that was during the day because office hours were from 8:00 to 4:00.  Getting those hours in between class schedules—you get those in barely.  You are stretching it.  I am literally running from one place to another.  At one time I put in sixteen hours a week because I still had to pay for school and being I was so far from my mother, calling my mom every day, "Mom, I need this; Mom, I need that," wasn't feasible.  My mother couldn't afford that.  Getting in touch with my father was kind of hard because he travels a lot, so I had to basically do it myself.  I learned you need to get money for your projects, money for your books, because projects in the education department—you have to make bulletin boards, posters, activities.  It gets to be costly and you have other things that you want to do and need to do.  You cannot live off of the food they feed you alone.  So, money was a necessity because I only made $60 every two weeks and that wasn't making it.*

*Actually, a lot of things have happened in my personal life that has been difficult. My dad died six days after my 21st birthday, and it was the Tuesday right before Thanksgiving. I found out when I got home. And, the very next week was the last week of classes, and I had exams that week, and then I had finals. And I had a 4.0 that semester until that point. I was completely devastated, and that was really hard but I just could not deal with it then. I had exams. I had to get A's. You know, I had to study. I couldn't think about it. Even that didn't stop me at that time. A lot of bad stuff happens, like at home or with my friends. I mean, I need to deal with what comes first.*

Points to Ponder . . .

1. What roadblocks have you encountered? How have you managed to deal with them? Have they had a significant impact on your performance? Have they affected your decisions or your goals? In what way?

2. Have you had to work while going to school? Besides the money, are their advantages to working while you are enrolled in college? What are the advantages? What are the disadvantages? Have you been able to limit your work hours so as not to cut into your study or sleep time?

3. Have you had major personal problems to face while in school? What have you done to help you cope with these problems? Have you considered using the counseling services on your campus to help you cope with personal problems? Find out where your counseling center is and what is involved in making an appointment

so that you are prepared if you should need the services. Research the other services of the counseling center? What kinds of support groups are available? Are there groups that deal with the range of personal problems, including those dealing with grief and loss?

4. Do you know where your health center is? Do you know what services are provided?

5. Have you been able to maintain a healthy connection with your family while managing to separate from them? Trace your progress in making your own decisions and choices?

6. Stress and fatigue can diminish optimism. How do you handle stress and fatigue? Do you have some strategies that usually work for you?

## The Lack of Faculty Support                    Chapter 18

---

## Introduction

As would be expected, every student had some negative features of their institution that they wanted to talk about or some negative experience to describe. A common complaint had to do with faculty. Although all these students had nothing but positive comments about the faculty they came into contact with through their developmental programs, that was not necessarily how they described their experiences with some other faculty. For every student who had some praise for concerned faculty, either from their support program or otherwise, there was another student (or the same student) who complained about lack of faculty support, especially lack of interest in student success. Poor advisement from faculty, or at least poor compared to the advisement they experienced from developmental educators, was another specific complaint. Although the experiences of these students may not be typical, especially given that they had a nurturing experience with which to compare, it is safe to assume that all students will find some identification with their complaints.

## Speaking of Which . . .

*I can say that I never felt connected with my department. I don't want to say that they are not there to help you, but their concern is not really for you as much as people would think. They are there to teach you and go home.*

It is funny because most of them are still in school too, and their job is basically to teach you but still be above you. I can't say I blame them. You can't worry about everybody and lose out on what your own goals are. That is understandable. But often you feel that they are saying, "I can tell you this, but don't bother me about it."

There are those professors who scare you. They come into class, they teach, and they leave. They don't offer extra time or extra support. If you are having trouble in the class and you have one of those professors that don't want to take the time, then you are not going to ask the question because you're scared, and so then you don't get your questions answered.

A lot of professors have the attitude, "Well, I don't care if you come." And you say, "Well, can I come by to talk to you?" And then they don't have the time, or when you have questions, they don't have the answers. They send you out to find the answers, and you're like, "Well, that's why I came to talk to you. I don't know where to go."

When I first started as a freshman, my advisor was hardly ever there for me. If I had an appointment with him, he would be going golfing or something. Eventually I asked for another advisor. My file from my old advisor wasn't even updated. It said I was still a freshman. At this point, I was a sophomore. He had nothing in there. Everything was just thrown around.

I think faculty is a big problem here just because they don't care. I mean, about anything. Usually, it is research, which is what I hear is the trend at most universities. As a

108

research university, they don't have time for their students. It is just that simple. I mean, I didn't get to know many professors, I got to know a few.

My classes are small compared to the rest of the university because of my major. This is a huge science school here—engineering, for example, and they have real problems. Most of my friends are in classes of 700 all the time. My economics class was 700-and-some people. It was like, "This is an auditorium. What is going on?" In those cases, your professor is usually unapproachable. When you try to approach them, it doesn't work. The graduate assistants become the ones, and even they are distant at times because they have so much work to do that it is ridiculous.

A lot of fault lies with some professors. I have gone to a number of professors and said, I don't understand this." And they say, "Well, that is your problem." So a lot of them don't have the skill to convey something in different ways.

Points to Ponder . . .

1. How have you overcome experiences of distance or rejection from faculty members?

2. If you haven't been successful in approaching faculty, asking for help outside of class, or making faculty aware of your existence, how might you change the situation? What would be the benefits of making the effort?

3. What suggestions would you have for students who are afraid to

ask questions in class?

4. In general, professors are interested in and enthusiastic about the subjects that they teach and in which they have spent years becoming knowledgeable or proficient. They are pleased to see that others share that enthusiasm. How might you use this theory to have your needs met by a professor in a given subject, especially if you are having difficulties?

5. Do you know your professor's name? Do you know his or her title? Office location? Phone number? Office hours? Can you expect your professor to know who you are if you have not even bothered to learn his or her name, answered a question, asked a question, or stopped to visit him or her during office hours? What can you do if your professor does not seem to be available for office hours?

6. What can you do to help yourself if you are in a university where class sizes are very large? Should you just assume that your professor is inaccessible? What are some other ways to learn the material or get your questions answered?

Lack of Interest                                    Chapter 19

---

## Introduction

In addition to the uncontrollable, fairly common obstacles to success that students faced, there were several students who described lack of interest in a particular subject or a required class as a difficult academic challenge.  In these cases, it was the disinterest more than the material that caused them to falter or fail.  On first glance, this problem seems to be out of character for students whose commitment kept them adequately focused on what they needed to accomplish. After all, it could be argued that, unlike developing an illness, developing an interest in a class is within one's control. Yet respondents described the experience as though they had no power to correct it.  And in one major respect that was true, since these were courses that they were compelled to take for one reason or another or with a professor that they could not change.  There were several such examples in which students brought up lack of interest in a particular subject or a required class as a distinctive roadblock to success.

Speaking of Which . . .

> *Yeah, there were some roadblocks, especially with classes that I didn't enjoy.  That is hard—to sit down and study for them when you don't enjoy, or when it is something that you don't really care about that is outside your major.  I think that was the difficult part—liberal studies, some of the, the English*

classes, the research writing class. I tried to put that off because I know I hate to write papers. So, that is one of the big things—not being excited about the subject. When you have to push yourself to do well.

Why I didn't do well in that class was because it was boring. The professor's style of teaching wasn't what I liked or that benefited me. It was strictly lecture, no visuals, anything like that. It was 8:00 am in the morning. I sat there for an hour and a half, and he just talked and talked, and I just sat there and wrote and wrote. And I wasn't interested in history per se, that type of era that we were talking about.

There have been some classes that I really wish I didn't take, that I really wasn't into. And there were some classes that I really enjoyed. Right now I'm taking photojournalism, and I enjoy that a lot. And I had short fiction last semester, and I got into that.

The first year your courses are more introductory and they aren't really interesting at times, and I just didn't want to go. And I was always tired and getting used to this place.

I can't do things that I am not interested in. I just can't really excel in anything like that. I mean, I can't get it. I mean, I can do it but it is going to be only so far—period.

Points to Ponder . . .

1. It is not reasonable to expect that students will be excited about every class that they take, especially if those classes are required to obtain the degree or as part of the major. You may feel

intimidated by certain subjects because you don't know much about them or because you have had bad experiences with a course in that subject previously. You may feel frightened of the professor or the professor's style, or you may be overwhelmed by the amount of work that is expected. These challenges are all part of the college experience. It is up to you to overcome such challenges and to make the most of them as opportunities to grow and to experience the satisfaction of having accomplished what might seem at first to be impossible.

Developing an interest in the subject, even forcing an interest, can go a long way toward improving your performance in a course. Creating that interest is up to you. How can you do that? Here are some examples that other students say have worked for them. See if you can add to the list.

- Sit in the front of the room.
- Focus on the professor and listen intently.
- Maintain eye contact with the professor
- Attend every class.
- Go to class prepared.
- Do all assigned reading before class.
- Take notes.
- Try to understand why the professor has an interest in the subject.
- Visit the professor during office hours and ask questions.
- Ask the professor to talk about how they developed an interest in their topic. Ask about their educational background and what made them choice this area. The professor will no doubt be pleased to talk about himself or herself and will find your interest to be refreshing. You will no doubt be remembered and should certainly receive the help you need.

- Immediately upon recognizing your lack of interest or your concern about doing well, seek out help. Visit the tutoring services, the learning center, the writing center.
- Attend any helping sessions that focus on the course, such as homework helpers, collaborative learning groups, supplemental instruction sessions. And keep on going.
- Talk with your advisor about your problem and ask for recommendations.
- Ask other students in the class for help.
- Ask upper-class students who have had the professor or the class for help and recommendations.
- Start your own collaborative learning group for the class.
- Find a study partner.
- Attend workshops in study strategies to help you manage the material in an effective way.
- Set goals for the course. Make them specific and think about them often. Dwelling on your goals, writing them down, talking about them—all this helps you to solidify your resolve and to accept your goals as doable.

2. Can you add to the above list? Perhaps others in your class can add some suggestions as well.

3. Pick three behaviors from the above lists that you are not currently doing. Write these behaviors down for a particular course that you are not terribly interested in or with which you are having difficulty. Make engaging in these behaviors your short-term goals for this course. Set short-term deadlines for accomplishing these three goals and then add three more to your list. Try these same strategies for all your courses.

## Difficulties for Minorities                     Chapter 20

---

## Introduction

The most compelling descriptions of negative aspects of the institution came from minority students in the study. With the exception of the Asian student (who described language and test taking difficulties), the seven African Americans and one Latino described having to overcome racial prejudices, negative attitudes, and low expectations regarding their potential for success. One student also talked about other forms of prejudice on his campus. Negative attitudes and behaviors came from faculty, staff, administrators, other students, and the institution's local communities. Interestingly, students' remarks emerged spontaneously, without any questions or reference from the researcher concerning their minority status or of its impact on their success. Just as interesting was the manner in which these students described their experiences. Though spoken not without passion, their remarks were spoken with an objectivity and maturity that underscored their success in dealing with these experiences. Their descriptions gave testimony to a high level of self-confidence and an ability to understand and deal with racism.

Speaking of Which . . .

*You have to be assertive and determined. It is hard to be on a campus a lot of times. I did not think the department* took me seriously. You are almost being told, "You are going not to be here next semester. Why should I go out of my way for you? You are a statistic waiting to happen." If you want to accept that you can, but if you just kind of say, "Well, you know, if that is what you think, I will see you the day I graduate." Unfortunately, that happened and it kept happening. And even though no one said it, you felt it. Questions were never directed at me until I raised my hand and asked, and said, "I know the answer. Let me tell you what I think." You have to earn your respect as a student on this campus. You can't just sit there because you are not acknowledged as a student immediately—at least some groups aren't. You know that you are not. I was determined to let people know that they will take me seriously. I am here like everyone else; my money is green too. And that is how when a professor would say, "Well, I don't have time for you." I took that as, "Your job description says you are to have time for me, you are not doing your job, so I will talk to someone else." You have to be willing to tell people, "Look, I am willing to learn."

I think the most negative thing that has happened to me has been more with professors, or not just professors—but people telling you or making you feel like you can't succeed or just trying to discourage you. I guess they are not really trying, but—I remember whenever I wanted to declare my major in public administration. I was speaking to one of the professors, and he was encouraging me to do the government major because it wasn't as hard as the public administration major. In public administration you have the accounting, you have the economics, and you have macroeconomics. With government, you have a lot of theory words. You know, it is not as analytical as public administration, and I knew what I wanted

116

to do, but I felt like he didn't know me. And I think that has been very negative. That has happened quite often.

I looked at other minority students. I am from small towns, predominately white, and this town is predominantly white, and the campus is predominantly white. But I was kind of more used to the situation than a lot of the other minorities because a majority of the minorities that come here are not from small towns. They are from large cities, and they haven't been in an atmosphere like this. And that in itself could devastate you your freshman year. And I didn't have to make that transition. That helped me, but my attitude didn't. And, I had to get rid of that. I had to realize that I had a problem first, and then I had to get rid of it or learn how to deal with situations better.

I am a minority here on this campus and sometimes it's difficult to find someone, professors or someone in that position—faculty members—that you feel comfortable with because sometimes you just do not feel like—well, I personally don't feel like I belong on this campus. It's not as diverse as it's supposed to be.

I went to an all black grammar school and in 8th grade I went to a predominantly white grammar school for one year. And in high school I went to a pretty much mixed school. Where I live is predominantly white, so it is no big deal to come here. A lot of other black students that came here, they have problems, and they had to stay, but it is no big deal to me.

There are a lot of things here that a lot of us don'tenjoy very much. The racial climate here is not very good. There are a small number of minority students for the size of the school. I usually pass for white, but it doesn't matter. You know, it is like a 7% minority here. But it is a very segregated school itself. You have the Latino community that stays with itself. Sometimes with the black community it is sort of the same. The Asian community, which is very large here in the grad school level--some people call it the Asian ghetto because their housing is university and it is sub-par—very, very bad. Mostly, I mean, everyone keeps to their own little groups here and the majority is white, so it's, it's kind of hard sometimes. I don't like to be in the Latino group, as a Latino because most of the people are Puerto Rican and I am not Puerto Rican so I don't fit anywhere.

I only know one person of my nationality here, so it is odd. Plus, the African American community is always trying to bring everyone into their community where I am not African either. But then a lot of my friends are. Then the white community—I have friends there, too. But here there is a lot of animosity toward each other. There are a lot of little groups plus, this past year there have been a lot of sexual orientation problems and sexual harassment.

My classes have been okay. But this past semester I have had a problem, a racial problem that I approached the English department with. My parents are immigrants. I have a whole entire class that talked about immigrants as if they are scum. Most of the class does it, and the teacher doesn't say anything about it. So, you know, I raised my hand, "Excuse me, but what are you talking about?" "They smuggle babies. They all smuggle drugs." And this is ridiculous!

I am on the student hearing board. Intolerance issues come up all the time. It happens too much. It is bad. It is not black and white necessarily. It is straight. It is everything.

*We had some minors beaten last year. Some lesbian girl was beaten by 20 people. It is the kind of thing that happens all over the place, but they say it doesn't happen here.*

*You never get a second chance to leave a first impression and you spend all your life developing a reputation, but it takes moments for you to lose it. So, it is like a lot of times, you know, people will come, and they will walk into class, you know, and something that may be acceptable in the city may not be acceptable here—pants coming off your butt, etc. You walk in the classroom; some teachers are intimidated by that. They see it on TV, etc. Immediately they label that student—"He or she isn't going to get anything outside of a C or a D in my class." And it makes it harder for that student whether they realize it or not. So, it is kind of important that we learn to paint a positive picture, and then once we paint that picture and we have established a positive and a mutual friendship and relationship with our cohorts or our professors. I say that because a lot of times I have been the only black student in my classes, and immediately students will take pot shots at me. But I will be quiet, and right before the class would end the teacher would ask a question, I would answer. And that will knock them off of their feet. That was just my way of saying, "Okay, you know, I am going to plant some seeds." And I get along with everybody, but a lot of times students should be cautious about the picture that they paint in the beginning and they don't. And it makes it harder for them in the end because if you came with a 68 or a 69 average, the teacher does not want to give you the benefit of those two. But if your character, you know, has proven something they can give you those two points. It adds to your success; it helps your ability towards getting good grades.*

Here at this university, I have had a few negative experiences with professors. I had an asthma attack—I am asthmatic—and this is definitely not the best place for anyone asthmatic. Anyway, I had a B in the class. The professor gave me an F. I had to go fight it and everything, and this was supposed to be a class teaching sensitivity. I had my hospital documentation, the doctor called and everything, but she made a judgement call, you know, on her own biases—not on my accomplishments, not on my achievements, but simply about the person that I am. And right now I am kind of happy because she looks like a fool. She saw me the other day eating dinner with the president at the country club, just him and me. So evidently, you know, she needs to be healed on the inside herself. And at first I was bitter, but I learned to get over those types of things. And I think that has added to my success in school because I don't necessarily walk into a classroom with chips on my shoulder.

Here in this town and at this university, I would say that the minority students take some heat from some faculty. Definitely! But on the flip side, here in town I have had some negative experiences too. I am an avid fisherman. I was fishing, and I ran across some of—I will just call them the Duke boys—and they, you know, were pretty nasty. But I picked myself up, and I walked away. You know, no need catching me in the woods hurt for no apparent reason. I believe that God is going to protect me at all times, right. And he will. But you need to be realistic too. You got to turn your cheek at certain times. Campus is very segregated. Unless you are a person that knows how to build bridges, that is not intimidated by a lot, and can present yourself well, you will tend to cling to specific cliques. The campus is very divided and it is my belief the administration facilitates that division. They need to have more

120

*activities and things to bring people together—especially when you look at the different Greek systems on campus and everything. Discrimination definitely exists, and there is no way of getting around it. It smacks you in the face. You are either going to be the type of person that is going to have a hand in making some decisions, or you are going to lay back and be governed by somebody else.*

Points to Ponder . . .

1. Have you ever felt as though you don't belong somewhere? That you don't fit it? Or perhaps that you do not measure up compared to others? How has this perception made you feel? How has it affected your performance or self-confidence? What did you learn from that experience about the treatment of others?

2. Would you feel comfortable speaking up against discrimination? Have you ever done so? Have you ever encountered a situation when you didn't speak up, but wished later that you had? Explain.

3. What advice would you have for minority students when they meet with the kind of discrimination that is described here?

4. Does your institution have programs that help people understand and deal with prejudice? Have you participated in such programs? Are they effective? Why or why not? What would you suggest be done to improve the situation of intolerance for minorities of any kind on your campus?

5. What is your reaction to the student's comments about the value of making a good impression?

6. How do you learn to "get over those type of things" as one student described his approach to discrimination?

7. How can you personally help to "build bridges?"

8. When it comes to affecting change, either for yourself or for someone else, how can you be "the type of person that is going to have a hand in making decisions" as opposed to the kind who will "lay back and be governed by someone else?"

Effort, Time Management, and
Other Study Strategies                    Chapter 21

---

## Introduction

When it came to identifying factors that contributed to their success, students talked about more than just abstract concepts like goals and commitments. They also described specific behaviors that they believed were important to their success. They especially described examples of effort, hard work, time management, plus a variety of other learning and study strategies.

Each student seemed to have at least one strategy that he or she felt had been particularly important—whether that was studying in a quiet place, taking good notes, being a good listener, making a schedule and sticking to it, reading every class assignment, or studying as though preparing for an essay test.

Students gave credit to their developmental programs for having taught them many of these strategies and behaviors. They described themselves as persistent, organized, and disciplined. They talked about relaxing, planning, and concentrating. One student described a strategy he used for building and maintaining his interest when he entered a classroom.

Mostly, students talked about applying hard work and effort, about striving to do their best, and about never giving up, because as one student concluded, "It is hard. I mean it is not a piece of cake."

Speaking of Which . . .

*Effort is really important, because sometimes you just feel like giving up. Things just get so hard. The classes that I didn't do well in—I think somewhere during the semester—I did give up on because at first I put forth all my effort and then it wasn't paying off. And then I was doing well in other classes so I just went ahead and paid more attention to the other classes than the classes I was doing bad in—which I should have done the complete opposite in. But I think in the classes that I have done bad in, I have given up effort because I know whenever we have pop quizzes or something—if I would have just studied or just looked over my notes a little, little bit I could have gotten an A on things. So, it is like, sometimes I didn't put forth all of my effort when I could have. Effort is very important.*

*You can't just get there right away. I think everybody is going to have tough times. Some classes are really easy. Some classes are really hard. But you got to want to try to strive to get that A—not just "Okay, I'm gonna do the bare minimum." You have to want to strive. I think it's about hard work—everybody has to put in a lot of hard work because if not, I don't think you are really going to achieve too much.*

*I would just sit down and plan my day. I was more organized—more time management wise, like actually setting schedules where I would study instead of just studying when I could study. I decided: this is when I'm going to study. It's not going to be a spur of the moment thing or a last minute thing—two days before the exam and say, "Oh, it's time to study." I* actually planned it ahead of time, saying, "Okay, I have a test on April 1st. Let's begin studying on March 17th." And just having that preparation. That way if I have questions I can go to the professor's office hours and talk to him during that time, set up group workshops where we can work together as a group from the class. So, it was a lot of team building, time management and just working closely with other people who were doing better than me. And talking to the professor. Finding different ways to study and interpret when I read. I went through assessment clinic to find out, "Is there something wrong with my short-term memory or my long-term memory?" And they found something wrong. So, it's like, "Okay, now what do I do to overcome that?" So that is another difficulty that I overcame. I learned I have to study more in advance and then like lag off a couple of days and then review like three days before the test to have it stick. It is like a preparation that is way in advance and then a very close review up until the test day. And it has helped in some classes and in other classes it hasn't because I am not interested in them and so I do poor, but I know I need to do better if I want to get out of here. So, I am working harder at the classes that I'm not interested in. There is only one class, though, that I am actually not doing well in. So, it's like, "I'm working harder to do that." I sit down and say, "Look, I can't make phone calls. I can't talk on the phone. I can't go visit people. I can't go to the movies. I can't go to the mall." And I am saying what I can't do, and realizing, "This is what I need to do," and I get it done. So, it is eliminating a lot of social activity and unorganized activities and unneeded activities that cause me to really sit down and focus on studying, preparing, asking questions, and I find that I am doing much better now than I was my freshman summer. This time I am interpreting it. I am writing questions for myself to answer, you know.  I am going about it in a different way.  And it is all through trial and error.

I would say the biggest factor is study habits though.  Good study habits are key—and I think I have developed good study habits.  Coming in as a freshman I know I didn't have very good ones, so I think that is one thing that I have developed in three or four years.

I would say an important factor is being prepared for class, pre-reading materials before going to class, actually setting time every night that is specifically for study time, and taking notes.  My note taking has become more efficient, I would say.  I started more in the outline form now whereas in high school I hardly ever took notes.  I think I have learned more to distinguish between important facts from stuff that isn't as important and learned to focus on them for studying for classes.

I think that I have learned that I have to be in a quiet place with no distractions, and I have gone to the library a lot of times when I know that I have to get this work done or I need to be able to concentrate on studying.  I would often just go to the library because I know that I can get my work done there.  So, it has to be a quiet, relaxed environment for me.

I try to be organized and manage my time for my different courses.  I have them all organized and know what's due and what's coming up and try to do the work that I know I have to do on time.

Grade-wise I would say that I took reading assignments seriously.  Other than just skimming them I always spent a lot of time doing the readings in any book. It made a difference. It made a big difference.

I have learned so much just by doing reading assignments. I didn't do reading assignments in high school, and when I came to here, the first thing I did was all the reading assignments. It made all the difference. I don't know if it's because I learned so much more from them or if it is just because it kept me in tune with school. It helped me keep a good focus on what I was studying.

There are certain faculty that I find interesting and others that I find not so interesting. But I'll walk into a class and I'll really connect to the professor to a point where I anticipate what he is going to say. And I pay attention to his movements—what he does to teach. It keeps me interested and awake.

Well, when I do my best I am pretty, pretty persistent. When I get an early start on something and start off early and start up in a relaxed mode—when I am in my best stride is when I am real methodical. When I am real methodical and I keep going, keep a regular pattern. Maybe for a week or so I have an uninterrupted schedule where I am doing this and this and certain hours in the night I am doing this and my sleep is regular and everything is going like clockwork. That is when I do my best. When I do my worst is when I have too many things at once to do and wait too long to do them, and I become rushed.

Time management. I am one of those types of people who likes to be on time. I have to watch with projects and papers that I don't get too lax.  With those I can procrastinate, but to be somewhere, I am pretty much there on time.

The big thing most freshmen say is important and hard is notes.  Most people don't know how to take notes.  They just write it all down.  I think if you can develop it early—your note taking techniques—you will be set because it took me a little while to find out that I don't take notes well.  I mean, I tried the whole-writing thing, write everything out and then do outlines.  Then, I have a laptop, so I started taking my notes on my laptop.  That actually is the best.  It helped organization.  I realized though that when I take notes; I just don't listen; I write.  And listening and writing doesn't help much, so I'll stop taking notes all together and listen.  I think listening is the key.

I guess I am very disciplined.  Each day I have this daily planner, and every day I write down everything that needs to be done that day, and I will not go to bed until it is all done.  Sometimes I am up very late at night because I have distractions, "Come do this," or "Let's go to dinner," or somebody will stop by.  So, you have to plan for little distractions and that means being very organized.

When I study for a class, I like to know it like it is an essay exam.  When I take multiple choice exams I like to not even finish reading the question and I know what the answer is.  I read it, and I know what the answer is, and I look for it.  I want to know it that well because I don't see the point in just studying for the sake of it.  And I know I put that pressure on myself.  Nobody else does.  I do it.

When I got all the syllabi from my classes, I would go through, and I would write down every date that something is due and that we had an exam. I would write it down in my calendar, and after I did that—after I wrote everything that was due down—then I would see which weekends I could go home.

I think that, if possible, some people should take note-taking lessons. For example if a professor has an overhead and stuff on, people just write that down and nothing else. They don't really know what to write down. I write down everything I can. That is why, if a professor mentions something and it shows up on an exam, I know it. And you need to go to class.

I don't let myself know that I am studying. If I am walking across campus or if I am sitting over there I have a book in my hand, you know. I am looking at a book or something, or I am talking to somebody—talking to a professor, talking to other students. I don't realize that I am always really studying as a part of my everyday activities. The only times I realize I am studying is for finals—when I force myself.

Points to Ponder . . .

1. What do you do when you feel like giving up? Do you have any strategies that work well to get you back on track and motivated to continue? Share these.

2. How do your study habits compare with those expressed here? How many of the strategies that are described by these students do you regularly use? Describe your favorite study strategies.

3. Do you have a particular study strategy that you would recommend to other students? Explain what it is you do, including how and why you believe it is a good habit to develop.

4. How do you prepare for tests? Why is it a good idea to use the strategy of studying for every test as though it is an essay test as one student here recommends?

5. What kind of reader are you? Do you make reading your assignments one of the priorities in your preparation for both class and tests? What does the student mean who talks about the advantages of reading everything, when he says that this practice "kept me in tune with school?"

6. Notice how many of these successful students engage in self-talk and self-monitoring. These two habits: a) thinking and talking about your goals and your plans and b) monitoring how well you are doing including analyzing what is working and what is not and why— both of these practices will not only keep you focused on your goals, but will constantly reinforce the habit of good study and hard work as the path to success.

7. Notice how these students talk about going the extra mile. For example, they are not satisfied with just reading, but with reading everything they can. They are not satisfied with just preparing for an exam, but in preparing as though they will know all the answers. They don't just take notes, but take all the notes they can—and they don't just attend class, they attend all their classes. These are examples of hard work. These are examples of applying effort. **Besides commitment and intention to succeed, the most significant factor in success, as described by these students who have learned how to do it, is EFFORT.** Hard work and

effort are not just empty words to these students; they are actually specific and meaningful behaviors.

8. Describe the ways in which you apply real effort. If there is more that you can be doing that you can not list as common to your habits and strategies, then you are not "going the extra mile." You are not applying real effort. What else should you do to "go the limit?"

9. If you do not have a plan for managing your time and if you do not make active and daily use of a planner, you are putting yourself at risk. One of the major reasons that freshmen fail or falter or drop out has to do with their inability or unwillingness to manage their time appropriately.

College schedules are different from any school or work experience you have ever had. There never seems to be enough time to accomplish all that is expected of you. Still, students can be lulled into believing that they have more time than they actually do, while missing opportunities for completing required assignments or preparing for tests. Added to those challenges are the many temptations to spend time on recreational activities or to simply waste time sleeping or socializing. In the end, students can become disappointed with their academic performance and still feel frustrated that there is not enough time for doing nonacademic activities.

The truth is that there is plenty of time to do both, if you set goals and use the proper tools to accomplish them. Going to college is like having a job. If you spend forty-hours a week on your "job" you will still have plenty of time to do other things. And like your job duties, your college classes and requirements should come first. The difference is that your forty hours will not be spent in a regular 8-hour per day format.  The freedom you have to spend your time wisely or not, coupled with the irregular hours of a typical college schedule, will require that you make a conscious effort to carefully plan your work.  Good learners do this on a large scale, always looking ahead at the whole semester, and on a small scale, planning daily and making the necessary changes to meet their challenges. **The most important tool you can use, therefore, is a planner that helps you to manage your time on a monthly, weekly, and daily basis. Buy one today!  Use it starting now!**

---

## Introduction

In addition to attitudes and behaviors regarding study and effort, students talked about the value of having a positive attitude, being determined, and making conscious choices. These attitudes and behaviors contributed to the ability of students to make academic goals their highest priority which, in turn, supported and nurtured the most important factors: the commitment to persist and the intention to succeed. With their academic achievement established as the highest priority, students were able to make appropriate choices on a day to day basis and avoid behaviors that might sabotage their primary goal. Setting priorities and making conscious choices demonstrated the level of responsibility they had assumed toward their education and their ability to take an active rather than a passive role in the learning process. Setting priorities, taking responsibility, and being self-directed learners were behaviors that set them apart from their less successful peers and also helped them avoid negative peer influences and other distractions.

Speaking of Which . . .

*I think it is all a choice. You can choose to study for a test or you cannot, and the consequences are whether you are going to get a good grade or you are not. So, I think it is more "I choose to study for this test." As far as projects, "I choose* to put all this time into this project because it is important to me." And, I choose to go to class because that is, you know, what I want to do. So, I think it is all a choice.

Well, I was just thinking about how I overcame not letting the social life bring me down. Once you look at what you want and what those organizations want, sometimes they are not the same thing and you have to choose one over the other. You just have to weigh things.

I used to let people make decisions for me, listen to the good stuff they had to say, and I'd said, "Oh, I'll do that." But that's what they would do and that's what they think I should do, or thought I should do. This is just one example, and it happened whenever I was deciding where to go for college. . . . I wasn't strong in math in high school and I wanted to be an architect when I graduated, so we went up to a university with that program. They had an open house, and we looked at everything, and I really, really wanted to be an architect. My mom—she didn't really discourage me, but she said, "If you are not strong in math you really shouldn't do it." I heard more negative from her about that choice than positive, so I just came to this school. When I got here, you know, I tried to do what I wanted to do from that point. There are so many things that new freshmen can do. You can go into any major. You can do anything with your life. It's just amazing, I think! So learning to make my own choices and be comfortable with that—it was a process.

Not allowing money to get in the way—or the idea of making a lot of money getting in the way of my choices for the rest of my life—allowed me to choose a major that may not be financially successful, but I will be happy.

It was in the summer and I went right up to the dean, and I didn't have an appointment or anything. And I said, "Look, I need to be in school. This dismissal letter is a mistake." And actually it turns out that there was two people with my name and they sent me his mail. But the truth is, I was dismissed, too. So I said, "Give me a chance, and I will be on the Dean's List." That summer I had an internship, and I had to do some things and take a couple of tests, and actually I did end up with a 4.0 that semester—in the summer. At that time, I was down and out, and it didn't take one minute to say, "I will fix this."

I know I took advantage of every resource that there was. That was a big thing for me. If you need help you are going to have to get it. You just have to ask and demand. When it comes to academics I am very demanding. If I want to know something, I need to know it. I went to a lot of professors and said, "Look, you didn't tell me this." If they didn't have time, I said, "When will you have time? I need to know this." That is just the way that I would approach things.

Although I had some bad times here as far as academics—being on probation, being expelled—I still persevered, and, for me, this has been my success—to persevere. They say college is the best years of your life. These have been the best years of my life because I have met a lot of people, I have done a lot of things, I have learned, not just academically, but about myself and what I can accomplish. You know, all that was mostly due to my motivation.

Being stubborn—that's what it takes. Because if I want to do something, I want to do it. That has been a wake up call, too, because when you come to school, you are used to doing what your parents tell you to do, and a lot of times you do what your friends are doing. But, like I am at school. I mean, I am paying this bill now. So, I can do what I want to do, and he, a professor, can't discourage me from taking another major, taking a step down when I can take a step up. I feel my chosen major is a step up because that is what I really want. But—I guess it is because I was stubborn.

Something that didn't help me from high school to college was insecurity—just being insecure with myself. And when you are insecure everything people say to you, you take to the heart, and then you get an attitude. So you're insecure, and you have an attitude. You don't succeed that way. A positive attitude is really important.

Once you come to an obstacle that you can't overcome you always have to take another route. Just try and try again.

You are here for school, and school comes first—first before the fraternity. And the guys in it now, they know that and they respect that. I have had guys in there who have a test, a paper due. They put it off. They go to a party, and they fail.

On the weekends I would just get my work done. I would do it. Or I would just go out one night, then Saturday and Sunday stay home and concentrate on getting my work done. We had study hours, too, in the library. So, I did my reading in there, too. I got a 2.8 that semester. So, you know, you just got to do it. Party in your free time.

Attitude is an important factor. As I get older I see how competitive things really are in the world. You might have to do something several times before you get it right. You have to be patient. If you want to reach a certain goal, you got to be patient. You can't give up. You try to find other ways around them roadblocks.

I will say that my attitude has helped me. I am very determined. Determination plays sometimes an outrageous role in my life in whatever I do. It helps me, but also it hurts me sometimes because I am determined to do so many things at one time. I sometimes find myself in a bind. But I'll get it done, because I am determined to do something else. I think I'm a very positive person, and I try to maintain a positive attitude no matter what I do. I always take a situation—be it negative or positive—and find something good about the situation to harp on instead of harping on the negative things.

My confidence level is very high. I would say one of my greatest characteristics or traits about myself is my self-confidence and my self-persistence. I am very persistent in the things I do. The confidence level is there; however, sometimes I disappoint myself because I try to do too many things at one time. When I can't do them the way I would like to, I think I am more disappointed than anyone else is. But I'm still confident. When things get tough and situations are hard and difficult, I always say I can do it. I can honestly say that there hasn't been a time where I just felt like I couldn't go on anymore. If I can't overcome it, I can go around it. Nothing is forever and the situation that is bad at the time won't last forever.

I knew it would work out. I never have any doubts about that from the beginning. I have never worried about money my whole life. I have had jobs where I have had tons of money and security and I didn't have 10 cents for a phone call. It doesn't matter. I just don't worry about it. I haven't starved yet, so why worry about it? What are you gonna do about it?

Determination makes me stay to prove to people that even though you said I couldn't do it, I should have gone to a trade school—no, I can do it. I can make it. No matter what you say, I can still do it. I have always been determined. When someone told me "no" that was something that I was not allowed to do, or "You can't do it because you are a girl," that would make me do it even more. Or, "You can't do it because you're not that smart." That would make me prove to them—yes, I can. I may not get 4.0s or 3.5s, but I can still do it with the highest QPA that is possible. I still do my best. My strong point is determination.

If I didn't want to do something I'd just tell them, "No." It was hard to say no sometimes. People wanted to go out or goof around, and I would just say, "No, I got stuff to do. I can't do it. Maybe later." Because if I went out and I didn't have my work done, I wouldn't have a good time anyway.

I don't really know what makes me successful. I think if there is something I want, I will do anything I can to try to get it—within reason. If that means getting up at 4:00 in the morning to study for an exam, I will do it. I want to graduate in the top of my class because I do eventually want to go to grad school. I just feel that a bachelor's degree isn't enough for me. I need more. Another thing that is important to me here at this university is because there are like 40 million people here. My dad always told me I would be just a number when I came here, and he tried talking me into going to a smaller school. Well, I will tell you that there are people who will not forget me when I leave here. I know my entire department. They know me, my name. And I think that is important, and if you can, like, single yourself out so you are recognized out of all of these people here, I think that is pretty incredible.

My determination came from within somehow. It wasn't anything that anybody ever put on me. I don't know where that drive comes from within. I really don't think I ever had it until I got in college—I did, but it wasn't as strong as in college.

I am very spiritual. I have a philosophy: on the right hand, if you don't have a high self-esteem you are committing suicide against yourself. And on the left hand, if you don't have faith, if you don't believe in God, that is homicide against God. So, if you are committing suicide on the right and homicide on the left and in the middle there is hopelessness. I refuse to be hopeless for anybody. I have been taking care of myself for a long time now—since the age of seventeen—and I refuse to be hopeless because hopelessness ultimately leads to the demise of oneself, and I refuse to go under.

I use negativity and turn it into a positive attitude. It is what I know best, to fight, to make the most out of opportunities, you know. I try to channel my negativity into a positive attitude. You got to remain positive because if you don't, failure to compromise ultimately leads to your own failure. So, I am looking to barter. If I have to take a little of this to get that, I do it.

*I just kept a positive attitude. I mean, that is what my dad taught me to do—to stay positive, don't be negative. You can't be down about everything in life. I mean, there are people worse off than you are.*

Points to Ponder . . .

1. Select specific examples from the students' own statements that illustrate each of the following attitudes:

   - Determination
   - Self confidence
   - Perseverance
   - Optimism

   Write a separate essay on each of the four attitudes listed above describing a situation in which you have displayed that same quality.

2. Select specific examples from the students own statements that illustrate each of the following behaviors:

   - Setting Priorities
   - Making Conscious Choices
   - Breaking Through Barriers
   - Developing Independence

   Write a separate essay on each of the four behaviors listed above describing a situation in which you have demonstrated the same behavior.

3. As learned behaviors, each of the attitudes and behaviors described here can be developed with practice. If you have not been able to identify at least one example of how you have displayed each of the attitudes and behaviors described here as positive influences on success and personal development, explore ways in which you can develop these skills. Share ideas with your classmates and friends.

4. Choosing the right major is one of the most common examples of college students' struggles with making choices. This struggle is to be expected. After all, one of the main reasons for being in college is to leave open your options as you learn about who you are and the possibilities that best suit you. And as one student described it, "It is a process." While that process unfolds, however, you must remain motivated to follow it through. And nothing helps with motivation more that knowing what you really want to do. As should be clear from everything that these successful students had to say about their own process, desire is a strong motivator. And motivation helps you to formulate goals and to continue reaching for those goals.

   To help you choose a major that you feel comfortable with and motivated by, find out what services are available in your institution to help you with this process. Is there a course you can take, a career center you can visit, some interest inventories you can complete?

5. If you are still struggling with choosing a major, perhaps you are trying to accomplish something that someone else has chosen for you—your parents perhaps. Or perhaps you are being influenced by what you read about concerning the current or future job markets. Although these sources may have the right answer for you, in the end, the only right answer is your own.

As a step toward finding your own best way, begin to analyze your decision-making abilities. Are you making conscious choices or are you making automatic choices? Are you leading your own way, or are you following? Making conscious choices in all the areas of your life, for which you are in control, will help you to develop self-direction and self-satisfaction. Even if the choice turns out to be one that you would prefer had been different, the important factor is whether or not it was your own.

Start with small acts of decision-making. Chart your progress. To help you in the process, make a list of priorities. If you can keep some preset priorities in mind, you will have an easier time of making decisions when you are faced with situations of pressure, whether because of time pressures or because of the influence of others. That way, if your decision has to be more automatic than conscious, at least it will be based on a pre arranged "automatic" choice.

## The Role of Attendance                    Chapter 23

---

## Introduction

Students had strong reactions to direct questions or probes about their opinions and behaviors regarding attendance at classes. Their position on this topic was clear: Without exception, students regarded class attendance to be one of the most important factors in academic success— for themselves as well as for other students. And, they backed their belief with action.

For some, going to class meant getting one's money's worth out of college. For everyone, attendance at class was the best way to learn, to gain knowledge, to know what was expected, and to stay on top of matters. Like monitoring their study behaviors and prioritizing their activities, class attendance was another demonstration of how these students took charge of their own learning, functioning as active rather than passive learners.

Speaking of Which . . .

> *My first roommate came up with a formula that every time you miss a class you spend so much money. I basically do not like to spend money.*

> *I felt cheated if I did not go to class. I felt so guilty when I did not go to class—incredibly guilty. I could not handle*

that guilt. That was way too much for me. I just said, "I will just go to class and do what I have to do." I can tell you that I have never fallen asleep in class. I cannot do that. I am always there—even if I don't want to be. You learn so much—maybe not from the professor—but you learn a lot from the people around you that are in the class. I think I learned a lot by sitting in class and watching other people learn. I taught myself to learn by watching other people around me learn. You take in from everything around you. I found out if I didn't go to class I missed opportunities, I missed gaining knowledge.

Oh, I've had very good attendance. I feel guilty if I miss a class. I would say I have missed maybe three classes my whole 4 years. When I talked to other people who don't go to class and then do bad, they don't understand. I think attendance has a lot to with what your outcome is.

One of the big influences for success is class attendance. I don't like when people complain about what grade they got and they never come to class. I think you miss a lot when you miss class because even if you do well on tests there are still things that go on in class that would benefit you. I know a lot of people are just here to get by and I want to get the most for my money.

I go to all of my classes. I will feel very guilty if I miss a class. And I'll feel as if I missed out on something. If I miss a class then I am wasting my money. Most professors, whenever they give a test, a portion of it is from their notes. Some professors use all of it on the test and none on the reading. The reading is more reinforcement. You can borrow someone's notes if you miss class, but to sit in and hear him talk about it and have him explain it is a different level. The writing and listening—they add an enhancement to your comprehension.

I think it depends on the student. Some students are like myself—they have to be at class. Other students—they can't make class because they went out the night before and they have people in the class who they have to borrow notes from. Some students can look at those notes and go from there. Now see, I think that is a downfall. I mean, if you can get a passing grade whenever you can get an A, well, I would go for the A. Why just get the passing grade?

I'm pretty good with attendance. I usually try to go to every class. Once in a while I miss a class. Here it's because the class size is relatively small, especially in political science. Attendance is really crucial because there is usually like a 10 or 15% participation grade. You really almost have to go on a normal basis to learn anything in political science.

Most of the time I am in class. Yes, I miss class—not a lot because I try not to have my grade affected by my attendance. And a lot of professors will do that. I am a tardy person—that is a weakness. I'm working on it. As far as attendance, for the most part, I am in class because most of the time I learn from being in class. I'm a hands-on learner. I could sit and listen to you and understand maybe if I do it better than if I sit and read about it. So, usually it is necessary for me to be there.

Just this one past semester I had to work a little part-time. It wasn't very smart because I had an 8:30 on Tuesdays and Thursdays, and I missed a couple of classes, and it kind of hurt me. I got a letter from my freshmen year because I took a computer class and I missed a lot. I had a roommate, and he was in the same class, and we tended not to go. That was like the first class of my day. I got a D in that class and I couldn't retake that my sophomore year.

My attendance in the fall is always better than in the spring. I get sick mostly in the spring because of my allergies. Attendance does help. For some teachers it helps a lot. You have to be there. If you miss a day, you are lost. Some teachers—they repeat what they say anyway, so it really doesn't matter if you miss a day or not. Teachers should never tell you attendance doesn't matter because no one will show up. So, attendance is important depending on the class and how the teacher teaches. It depends on how you learn. For me, I need to be there every day regardless.

My attendance record is pretty good. I mean, I am no saint. I missed a couple classes here and there, but the only time I really miss class was like to do work for another class— like study for a test. I like to get information directly instead of—like if I asked you what went on in class, you would tell me, but it wouldn't be the same thing. So, you might miss something little that is so important. So that is why I always went.

You don't have to go to class at here. Usually, I mean, sometimes you do, but nobody goes. You don't know how big your class is because you never see everybody. Professors are angry about it. But it's foolish not to go. If you go and pay attention you are fine. I mean, at least if you don't study you have an idea about the test. You're not going to get an F; you will at least get a C.

I think going to class is important. You can get the notes, and, yeah, you can spew it out, but do you really know what it means? I mean, you have memorized it, but, so what?

I have not missed a class since my very first semester here. I have not missed a single class. Everybody is like, "No." Well, I know people that don't go, "Oh, it's raining, I don't want to go to class today." Now, of course, I have gone to every class, but I might not have paid attention all them time. I have fallen asleep in a couple of classes but I was there. I think it is important.

You have to go to class. I mean, I hate going to class a lot of times. When it is 25 below zero I do not want to go to class! Okay, but I really think you have to. You get so much more out of it. If you really are here to learn, you have to go to class. I have gone sick. I had pneumonia this semester—I did—and I went to all my classes. I would bring in a box of tissues or a roll of toilet paper, and I would sit there. And I remember I was taking this one exam, and I was dying, but uh, I was there, you know.

Points to Ponder . . .

1. Successful students know that the greatest single factor in success in any single course is ATTENDANCE. Just being there works! What are the more obvious reasons why? Look at the students' explanations to draw up a preliminary list.

2. Supplement the above list with some reasons of your own. In other words, identify all the advantages you can think of for maintaining good

class attendance.  Now list all the disadvantages you can think of.  Which list wins the sensible, thinking person's choice?

. Do the following exercise.  Take the cost of tuition, fees, and room and board to keep you in college for one semester.  Divide that total by the number of hours you are scheduled to be in class that term.  In other words, if you have 5 courses for 3 credits each, or 15 credits, you would normally be expected to put in 15 class hours per week.  Multiply your class hours by the number of weeks in the semester.  This amount is what you have paid for each hour of class.  The next time you choose to miss a class, picture yourself tearing up, burning, or otherwise destroying that money.

Carry this thinking one step further: Suppose you fail that same class.  Repeating it means paying for it all over again.  Suppose you get a mediocre or low grade when, by attending, you could have gotten a much better grade.  Did you mean to pay for a mediocre grade?  Do you buy sneakers, throw them away, and just keep the box?  Do you pay top price to buy defective sneakers?

The next time you choose to miss a class, remember this: American college students are the only consumers that are happiest when you don't give them what they paid for.  That's a clever generalization.  But does it fit you?  Are you happier when class is cancelled or ends early?  Are you happier not attending the class for which you are in one sense a consumer?

Starting now, why not make it your goal to not miss a single class.  With that challenge as your goal, you should come out very well in the end when it comes to your attendance record.

As Woody Allen is quoted to have said when asked the question: To what do you attribute your success?  "JUST SHOW UP."

## The Role of Ability                                    Chapter 24

---

## Introduction

Students were asked to comment on the role of ability in success.  It is of interest to know how these students perceived the role of ability in academic success, especially since it was measures of ability, like placement tests and SAT scores, that had marked them as high-risk students.  Not surprisingly, students minimized the role of ability in academic success, particularly compared to the influence of other factors such as hard work and effort.  They regarded ability as an advantage (a kind of strength), but it was effort (as manifest through hard work) that they believed essential to success, with or without ability.  As one student put it, "I don't think we know our abilities."

## Speaking of Which . . .

I know my ability to do a lot of things was not considered to be top rank.  I was told many times that you do not have the mind to do this type of thing.  A lot of testing, learning disabilities and things like that—that is fine.  But you can't see any kind of cognitive thing, therefore, you cannot tell me what is not going to work in my mind.  You can't measure it.  Cognitive ability is unmeasurable.  If that is the case, that ability can be measured, then kids say, "Then everything is out of my ability."  If you are going to think about it constantly then you are going to do it.  To tell someone that they can't do anything or that their ability is slight—I have always believed that there is nothing that I cannot do. And there is nothing anybody can't do. If you have the mind set—you are willing to take maybe the consequences of failure—you can do it.

I think ability does have a lot to do with it, but somebody who does not have as much ability, as say the person sitting next to them, I think it comes down to hard work again. They can get the help. And I know that it is not going to be as easy for them, but if they want to do it and they set a goal for themselves, then they can achieve it. It is kind of discouraging, though, when you see someone who has high ability and they waste it while you are working hard.

I think that ability is important if they know what strengths they have—what they can do and what they can't do, but whenever you know that you are not strong in an area it is not good then because sometimes it discourages you from doing things. You should be open-minded with it. Don't constrict yourself and confine yourself just to things you can do.

I mean it could be the style of learning or the style of the professor—the teaching. Like certain styles are harder for me. I am not a choice-maker. I mean if you ask me an essay question I will do much better on an essay than multiple choice. And I mean it was the same with SAT scores. I did very poor, but in college and otherwise it has been tested and stated that if you have a high SAT, you will likely succeed in first year of college. I disagree with that.

I think you need to have a certain amount of ability—the ability to try and try again and the ability to actually not give up. But if you put your mind to it, I think you can succeed. I have come to certain subjects where you know your limits but you also know how far you can succeed within that limit. Sometimes you may hate something, but if you try it you never know—you may like it after all. Like, as a child I was in placement for LD reading. And reading now is my minor. And I mean, I figured, if I am going to be a teacher and I struggle in reading—if I pick it up as a minor at least I will be strong in it and overcome weaknesses. You kind of have to overcome it by taking courses or whatever.

Well, it all comes down to a lot of hard work—more than ability. I have had ability all my life. But if I chose not to do anything with it, I never did anything with it.

I always looked at myself as not really having a lot of academic ability. Like, I concentrated more on working hard. I know some people that get much better grades than I do that don't work hard because they don't have to—which is good. I mean, I wish I was like that, but I know that I don't really have the same ability, but I work hard and get good results from that. So, I just have to work harder than other people do. Does it matter as long as you get to the same place?

Points to Ponder . . .

1. Are you an independent learner? Often times students think that other students have some special expertise or ability. You know the common responses. You may have used them yourself: "He's a good writer; I'm not," or "She has a math mind; I don't." In fact it can be argued that the good writer and the good math

mind have no more ability than the next person does. They simply have more skill. They have learned to be good writers or good math minds through interest and practice. Successful students are what can be called self-directed, independent learners. They work with things that they can control—factors that actually improve their results. The following are good examples of things that good learners use to improve their thinking skills:

- They PLAN WORK. Good learners do this on a large scale— always looking ahead at the whole semester—and on a small scale—planning daily and making the necessary changes to meet their challenges.

- They MONITOR AND SELF-EVALUATE THEIR WORK. They engage things like testing or checking their learning as they study, reviewing the results of tests and papers, and being honest with themselves about their efforts.

- They USE FEEDBACK TO IMPROVE PERFORMANCE. They examine feedback available to them from different sources— tests, professors, advisors, friends, relatives, themselves.

- They PERSIST. They don't expect it will always be easy. The habit of persistence is a good one, because it will always lead, at the very least, to SELF-SATISFACTION—and good students have that feeling over and over!

What other secrets do successful students have? They have certain feelings that work for them rather than against them. You can develop these same feelings, especially if your are working on the performance skills listed above. Successful students have learned to feel the following:

- SELF-MOTIVATED

- SELF-CONFIDENT

- SELF-CONTROL

In addition, good learners regulate their basic self-messages. This means they are in the habit of telling themselves positive things about their abilities, avoiding any negative messages, while still being honest about their effort and the role of hard work.

Good students also VALUE GOOD LEARNING.

And good students are SELF-REWARDING—they treat themselves. BUT FIRST THEY EARN IT!

Now you know the "secrets" to success. Spread the secret!

2. Now that you know the secrets of independent learners—What kind of learner are you? Evaluate yourself against the factors listed and described here? Make it your goal to complete the picture of the good learner and the active learner by practicing any of the skills you are not currently using.

Personal Failure                                    Chapter 25

---

## Introduction

Students directly addressed the role of failure in their college success: their reactions to it, how it influenced their attitudes and behaviors, how they dealt with it, the importance to their ongoing growth, and its impact on their goals and commitments. The students' perspective on the value of effort over ability was confirmed by their comments about failure, their own failures as well as the failures of others.

Many of the students talked about using failure to promote success, of learning from their mistakes, of engaging in behaviors that showed they were in the habit of viewing failure as something controllable and situational—if not in the short run (after all, some faculty could behave like "jerks"), at least in the long term ("I'll take the class over").

When it came to discussing failure, two notions emerged consistently: (1) failure was viewed as a learning experience and (2) the antidote to failure was regarded to be effort. As one student explained it, "F doesn't stand for failure, it stands for feedback. This means I need to switch gears." Students did not blame someone else for their failures, and when they did blame themselves, it was not in a way that destroyed their self-esteem: "You can't pick a failure to define your worthiness to go on. Failure in anything doesn't define who you are. It can make you sit up and smell the coffee, though."

When they experienced some form of failure, students did not view the event as outside their control; they did not see the circumstance of the event as unchangeable. On the contrary, they made realistic qualifications, ones which motivated them to correct the problem—to be motivated to do better the next time.

Instead of giving up, they made accommodations in their behaviors or sought any number of solutions. Some used failure as an aid in recognizing their real interest and changed their major as a result. Some took a failed class over with a different professor and worked harder. Most sought help from others, especially counselors, coaches, tutors, and other learning resource personnel from their developmental programs.

In the end analysis, everyone used failure as a means to strengthen the commitment to succeed. The crises they experienced as a result of coming face to face with failure were opportunities to come up against the true strength of their resolve to succeed.

Speaking of Which . . .

*It just feels good now that I know that I've got seven weeks left. I am ready to go. I had to ask myself, "What are you going to do next?" So, I know what I am going to do. I have my plans all mapped out. I am just ready to do it. Whether I succeed or fail at that point, it will be okay, because I know that I can get through because I have done it already. I have succeeded. I have failed. I have succeeded. I have failed. It's like a roller coaster ride, but yet I am still coming out on top because I am succeeding again. And then there will be more failures, but you know, you just keep pressing on to succeed.*

I think what helped me reach my goal of academic success—one of things that I always think helped me, believe it or not—was failing, because I learned so much about myself when I failed. I learn more about myself when I did bad on a test than when I did good. When I do good I just kind of throw it off and say, "Well that's fine." When I fail I have to look at myself and say, "Wait, why did I get this grade? Do I deserve this grade? Do I know anything about what I am talking about?" And if I said, "No," then I had to look at myself and say, "Well, make sure you don't do this again." You have to know why you did this. So, what helped me succeed, I think, was failing, because if you could take failing and bounce off it, then that is success. Every time I failed, I still got back up. And it taught me about a lot about myself, and how my personality is, and how I need to shape my personality in order to achieve a goal.

I know the first time I failed. I will never forget this time. I have been a musician since I was age two. I came to college, and the first class I took was a music class. Now, I thought I knew everything that there is to know about music, no problem. That is an easy A, I thought. The first test I took was all about music and how to write music. I failed it. "How am I going to explain this to anybody?" That was my very first college test. I failed it good. The professor said, "Well, at least you were consistent. You didn't get anything right." And then I took it again and got 100%!

I was so excited to have my first college test. Then I got an F on it. I remember coming to my educational counselor and saying, "Look, I failed this test." She said, "I don't know; maybe you are just nervous." "How do you know that I am nervous?" "Well, you spelled your name wrong." That was a lesson, too. Everything I looked at as hard-times was really a lesson. I learned how to overcome things, and the quicker you learn to overcome things the better you are. There are so many instances that happen academically that if you dwell on them, it will just pull you down. I can get a bad grade now and say, "Okay, it's bad." And that is that—end of it—but before, I would dwell on it, and negative thinking got me nowhere. I had to learn to forget about them because it is not healthy. Everybody has stress. I just learned how to deal with it.

Most people think that failing is negative. Failing is actually a positive when you really want to think about it. If you never fail you won't be able to teach someone else. But if you fail things, it is going to be a little easier to relate to situations and things. And that all comes from staying focused.

Mostly I dealt with failure through counseling—going to counseling here and talking to someone who didn't know me who would have an hour just to sit and listen. When my grades started slipping, I was just freaking out. I was scared. I was panicking. "I can't tell my grandmother that I am not doing well. I can't tell my mother I am failing." When I got expelled it was like, "I am going to hide this from everyone." I am just going to say, "Well, I will go to the summer school," and just do, you know, whatever, and then tell them that I was reinstated because I was trying to look at it in a positive way—like this is a learning experience for me. I think it was a learning experience for me, to recognize that although I have the support, the backing, a lot of people who are encouraging me, I can still fail and come right back and do the same thing again and pass.

My first semester I didn't do as well as I expected, and right then I learned that I have to put in time in college. I can't just get by like I did in high school. So, I think that was the biggest factor that opened my eyes and I, you know, said to myself, "Look, I'm going to have to put in the time here if I want to succeed." So that is when I actually started setting time aside for my studies, learning to manage, cutting out things, looking to priorities, you know, what is important.

I don't think failure really affected me. I kind of looked at it in the point of view "I can't do well in everything. Just because I did bad in this one class does not mean that I should not be in college and I'm not going to succeed." So, I think I have looked at it with that point of view—not to put myself down or get myself down for future years or future classes. It was just one class out of my whole college career.

Well, it's not just about success, but success and drawbacks because they really wake you up, too. Just like with classes. There have been classes that I have done so badly in, and it has been so stressful because I would study and study for a test and then I would end up getting a bad grade. With economics, I studied so much and I felt like my time and effort was worth more than a C, you know. Those things wake you up, too. They weren't really successes, I don't think, but learning how to go to the learning assistance center—you learn how to talk to your professors and—don't wait till the last minute. I would say successes **and** failures are what influenced my success.

My first two years, I was kind of in that social thing, adjusting thing, but I knew I wanted to succeed. I knew academics were important, but it was just so rocky, and then I just woke up. I don't know how it happened. I am glad it happened. But just all of the sudden I realized—I have to get

159

on the ball. I think it was my accounting—managerial accounting class—I took. I got a B on my first paper and it was the first time that I got a B in accounting and that just pushed me. It made me feel like, "I can do this." You know, all the time I was thinking, "I'm not good at math," or "I'm not good at this—not good at logically thinking," or whatever and that attitude was like taking over what I was doing. It really was. I didn't realize how strong it is because if you are positive—I was just always negative toward math so of course I wasn't going to do as well as if I had a positive attitude. After that B, I think that semester my grades have been coming up because I have been looking at it totally different than I used to look at it.

When I first entered my freshman year, my idea was that I wanted to be a psychologist. I have always liked mind-work, and I have always liked to help people do things, and I like to observe people. And after my first year of general psychology, I got a C, and I kind of rethought it. I shouldn't have let that stop me, but for some reason, I changed my major. I mean, I figured I work well with kids, I like kids, and I am very patient. I talked to one of the summer school professors. When I went back to my high school I talked to one of my teachers and they said, "You will be a great teacher."

I went to seek help. I didn't give up—no, I didn't. I know that I took music, and my first time I got a D, too—intro to music. I took the same professor the second time but I got compact disks instead of tapes, because we had to listen to the music to pass. I got a B the second time with the same professor. I mean, I spent more time on it. Plus, like I said, the CD and the tape—it makes a big difference because you can skip. You don't have to spend as much time rewinding. I also adapted to the changes to the best of my ability and if I couldn't succeed, I have always adapted very well to things, and I have also gone with the flow of things.

Another one of the keys, I think, is always to know your interests. I think you need to just sit back and go for a walk and just reflect on your strengths and weaknesses and your interests.

You try to find other ways around the roadblocks like with sports and stuff, like with basketball. Sometimes if you're not doing well in the class, you just gotta change the way you study or your approach to it.

I was not in the class from the start, so immediately I fell behind. I went over to the learning skills center and spoke to the lady in charge of the tutoring services. I asked her who I could get to work with me. I sat down and worked with the tutor. I also went to see my professor several times and he tried to help me, and, unfortunately I was too far behind. I kind of gave up. I could have done better, and I put all of that on me. Statistics is a difficult subject, however I feel as though if I had been paying attention from the start, I would have been fine. I had to repeat it. I was tutored several times but once I saw that I wasn't going to get it, I didn't want to waste their time and continue. The tutor asked me how did my class turn out, and the lady in charge asked me, and my academic advisor also asked me. I had to explain to them what happened. So, he advised me when would the best time be in my schedule to retake it so that I wouldn't be behind.

Getting a grade I thought was, you know, less than what I had expected to get, I would look at the grade and think, "Why did I get this grade?" And you read the comments, and you're like, "It doesn't make sense." So, I'll go to the professor and be like, "Can you explain this grade to me?" And they will give you some kind of explanation about why it happened or whatever and you're like, "Well, okay. They justified it." Then I just say, "Well, alright. I didn't do that well then," and set it aside and go on with other things. I never come out and dwell on it more than a day. If they don't justify it enough to satisfy me, then I say, "Alright then. If there is a better grade you just don't want to give it to me." And then I put it aside—don't dwell on it. Just go on the next day and make sure I do better next time and make up for that grade. If I can get it changed so that it doesn't hurt my final grade, then I'll get it changed. If I can't, then I will try harder.

I was real upset about not doing well in a class. I attribute my failure to not taking very good notes in class.

There have been one or two classes that I didn't do well in. I don't blame it on the professor. I put more of the blame on myself.

I had to take a couple of courses over. It was due to procrastination. Definitely. Nothing else.

You can't pick a failure to define your worthiness to go on. Failure in anything doesn't define who you are. It can make you sit up and smell the coffee, though. You can take it over—no big deal. The first time I had to take a class over I was crushed. It was the best thing I ever did. The best thing I ever did was have a hard instructor that gave me a hard time and wouldn't let me slide on anything and had no mercy. Thank God for him. I learned not to get behind, I'll tell you that!

When I took it over I got an A in the class, and I understand the concept—I understand organic chemistry a lot better.

It was biology. I got a D the first time, and I still thought I wanted to major in it. So, I took it again the next semester, and I got an F the second time. It was just because I lost interest and never went to class or anything. So I still feel bad about that, about just giving up, but it is just one class. It did teach me something. That summer I changed my major because I just knew—I knew that I really didn't have—it is kind of hard to describe—I didn't really like science to begin with, and I knew that I would have to take it for four years.

It really hits home whenever something bad happens and you are on the verge of failing. But when you are one the verge of being thrown out of school, then you realize that that desire is still there. It was just misplaced for a little bit.

I think it all started my spring term. I wasn't concentrating on learning my stuff for school. I was more concentrating on learning my stuff for the sorority. I really didn't apply myself at all. I mean, I would be lucky if I made it to the class, let alone participate in class or hand in things on time. I got myself into this rut where I didn't know what to do. I got my mid-semester grades and they were all Fs. I was carrying 15 credits. They were all Fs. My parents were disappointed because my grades got sent home to my house, and they were just like, "What are you doing? What is this pledging thing all about?" I don't think it was so much, just the pledging thing that had something to do with it, but I just didn't have any desire. I just felt like I didn't want to do anything. I just felt like weak. I just wanted to, you know, lay around, sleep, go out and have fun, party all night-type things. I had this sense when I failed of like, what am I doing?  What am I thinking? My parents are spending the money to send me here.  I was trying so hard my first semester.  Then I just slacked off.  It didn't really even matter to me at all.  I was just like, "Academics—oh well.  I gotta pledge.  I gotta get in.  I gotta feel like I am wanted."  And I kept thinking, "Was it the sorority or was it just me not wanting to do the work?"  I realized I had to turn myself around.  But, it wasn't a good feeling at all.  There was not desire.  There was nothing there.  After I failed, after I got all Fs, which was awful—I cried a lot.  I realized, "Hey.  You got to settle down and relax."  I realized I had to straighten myself out because right there I just blew twelve or thirteen credits right down the drain.  That was how much money I spent.  I realized, "What am I doing?  I knew I couldn't be in 15 different extracurricular activities while trying to pull my grades up.  I knew I had to limit myself to what I could do and apply myself to that one thing giving 100%.  And I knew at this moment it wasn't, you know, going out to parties.  I knew it wasn't participating in organizations on campus.  I knew it was my academics.  And I had to settle myself down.  I had to realize that I had to grow up and I had to achieve this goal.

Economics killed me. Second test—I went home because it was my birthday, and he gave it to us after Easter Sunday, and I failed that test.  I didn't study at all.  Then I said, "You know, I have to take that class over because I need it for my general study stuff."  I was like, "Oh, God.  If I fail that test it means that I am going to be really low at this point," so I studied for about two months straight.  Every night I studied, even though we didn't have any other tests, we had one last final.  So, I just studied straight through, and I don't know exactly what I got on it but I ended up with a B minus in the class, so I must have got an A on the freaking final.  I was like—

that was fun.  That was the one time I got it in gear, but I should have done that for every class.

My first semester I thought I was going to fail math.  I was stupid for taking it.  I was so lost from day one—and I had calculus in high school.  But my teacher didn't know how to teach.  I got up here and I was totally lost and I had no idea until I stopped going to class.  But, I went to the math-tutoring center instead, everyday.  And I failed every exam, and at the time I just really wasn't adjusting well to this college, and I really didn't care.  Like, I didn't want to fail.  I just wanted to get a C.  I thought I needed a C to get credit for it, but I only needed a D—thank God.  I just wanted to pass because I didn't ever want to have to take another math course as long as I lived.  And, when I got my grades, I didn't show my parents my grades, and I was so upset.  I was devastated.  I just didn't want to be here.  I didn't feel like doing anything.  I was like, "This is NOT acceptable." So, I basically—the next semester I locked myself into my room and I didn't do anything.  I didn't talk to anybody and I just studied.  That is all I did.  And I got a 3.73 that semester.  And it brought my GPA up.  Each semester I get a higher GPA, and it brings it up and, so, I got my 4.0 last semester.  I missed it last fall, 3.95, I had all As and an A-minus.

F doesn't stand for failure; it stands for feedback.  That means I need to switch gears.  As a matter of fact I can tell you this, if you take all the F's that I had, they would equal a semester of school, but I'm graduating.  One may say failure, but I say success because I am finished.

Points to Ponder . . .

1. Are you bored, angry, frustrated, overwhelmed? Do you find yourself thinking things like, "I'm a failure! I can't do this. This course stinks. I can't study . . ."

Most people believe that thoughts like these are a result of how one feels. After all, you decide, "I can't control my feelings."

Actually, quite the reverse is true. Your feelings are a result of how you think. And you <u>can</u> control your thoughts!

Think about it. Don't your moods change depending on what you are thinking? Don't different people seem to have different feelings about the same experience or situation? Haven't you? It all depends on what your thoughts are telling you.

Try this. The next time you find your thoughts giving you negative messages, write them down in one column that you label "Emotional Reactions." Then answer these thoughts in another column you call "Rational Responses." For example, some rational responses to the emotional messages above might be, "I may have failed this test, but I'm not a failure. I do plenty of things well. Look at all I've learned in this class. I'll get some help to figure out what I can change to do better next time. There will be a next time."

Do this exercise for 15 minutes each day for your negative messages about anything. If you find yourself complaining too much and problem-solving too little, try this exercise. Fifteen minutes a day will quickly pay off. You will fell better and be better. How do you feel? It depends—how do you think?

2. To what do you attribute your failures?  Pick a time when you have failed at something, made a mistake, or didn't do something as well as you wanted?  Analyze why that happened and explain.  If you explained the reasons to yourself at the time, what did you do next?  If not, what should you have done?

3. How do explain your failures to yourself, in general?  Do you believe that your failures of performance are an evaluation of your self-worth, or just of your performance?  What's the difference?  Explain.

4. If a failure is your fault, what do you do about it?  If the failure is not your fault, what do you do about it?  Are you able to tell the difference?  Is the failure sometimes a result of both conditions?  Give an example from your own experience.

5. Describe how a particular mistake or failure has ultimately led to something positive for you.

---

## Introduction

Students expressed opinions about the behaviors and motivations of other students who had not been successful and had either failed or dropped out. Generally, when they expressed their opinions about the lack of success of other students, they were referring to students in general. At other times, they were commenting on students who, like them, had entered college through a freshman support program, but who, unlike them, had failed to graduate, even with the kind of support they themselves had valued as freshmen.

When they commented on the failure of others, their remarks echoed the same themes they had used to describe success, only in reverse. Students viewed the failures they had witnessed in others as resulting from a lack of commitment and self-direction; an unwillingness to make academic success a priority; and a lack of concern, drive, or ambition concerning educational goals. They saw failed students as being followers instead of leaders, being passive rather than active, making poor choices or no choices, and engaging in self-defeating behaviors.

In short, they believed that students failed or dropped out because of the absence of a strong desire, commitment or intention to succeed. In no way did they see these failures as having to do with a lack of ability. It was effort that made the difference—what you <u>did</u>; not what you were. As one respondent put it, dropouts and failures did not <u>fail</u> out of college, they "<u>fell</u> out."

Speaking of Which . . .

*I think that a major problem with a lot of people on college campuses is that society tells you that you need a degree, but individually you have to know why you need it. It doesn't make any sense to do something that someone told you to do, because then you will say, "Well, I got it, and I don't know what to do with it." So, I have a degree. I still may not know exactly what to do with it, but I have a pretty good idea—a better idea than I had before. I think this is a problem that everybody has at some point in time—"Why am I here? What is this going to do for me?"*

*I think most students are goal-oriented and some are just job-oriented. They don't want a career. They just want to get a job. They just want to get by. I want a career. I want to be successful in something, not in a bunch of things. I want a career where I can settle down and know what I want to do. I want to work with people. I want to deal with children. I know exactly what I want to do. So, most students who come to college are successful because they want to be successful. They have a field that they want to work in. And they have a goal that they want to achieve. Some people just come because their parents make them or just to get away from home. And then they don't do well, and they say, "Hey, I can just go back home."*

It has a lot to do with the person, the individual. I can't speak for every individual, but the ones that I have talked to, mostly it is their friends that influence them and they just don't want to be here. This is just a way to get away, to get away from home. It's like, "I'll go to college and say I've been there, but I haven't done it. I didn't complete it." You came, but you saw, and you didn't conquer. I mean, "Why come then?" You are wasting a lot of people's money and time and a lot of people put effort into helping these individuals get out and do better in school, but they don't want to help themselves. That is the difference between them and me. I want to get out of school. I want to be successful. I want to accomplish goals in life, you know. And they just don't.

I think it is mostly a matter of choice. If you want to succeed you are going to have to put time aside. I mean, college is so much different from high school. As, you know, it is like—big freedom. And you have to have self-discipline. It is your choice whether you want to stick to the studying or do other things. You have to set your priorities.

I think the students that come through the developmental program already come through with a negative attitude. Like, "I'm not a success, and I'm not going to be a success because I have to be in this program." And I say to them, "That is not true." They come in with a negative attitude like, "I gotta be here in the summer! My grades were not great in high school. What makes you think that I'm gonna be any better here?" You know, they just don't try. They don't want to be here. Most of them come just because they got accepted or they want to get away from this city or that city or wherever—move out of mom's house, get some responsibility, and then they don't take it. They don't want to try. So, it is

171

*not the program that is failing them. They are failing themselves.*

*You know, I hear freshmen all the time talking about what they are going to do over the weekend, but I never hear studying. And I always ask them, "And when are you going to study?" "Oh, you know, I'll get to it." "But when? You are talking about this party you are going to, about this outfit that you are going to buy, you want to be a part of these fashion shows." I think they need to eliminate a lot of things that they have activity-wise until people's grades get up. They should be told that this is the criteria. You have to have a 2.0 to be involved in the fashion show, or to be involved in Miss This or Mr. That, or some fraternity or sorority—whatever.*

*They don't succeed because they don't want to. They don't try. They allow their friends to influence them. They keep negative company, and when you keep negative company that brings you down.*

*Procrastination—I think that is a big thing. I see people waiting until the night before to do projects, and when you wait that long you are not going to do as high-quality of a project as someone who has started a couple days or a week ahead of time. Maybe they don't care about what their quality of work is or maybe they don't have the time. Maybe they have other things in their life going on. Maybe they have the attitude that "If I get by, I am just floating through college. If I can just get by I am still going to get the degree that somebody who put all this work into is going to get." I think those attitudes are what a lot of those students have.*

*Some people, when they come to college—and it is not just the program, it is all students—when they come to college they really aren't thinking about their future. They are thinking about other things like their extracurricular activities, the friends that they need. And that is really, really overwhelming because you are in a totally different situation. And yeah, you are supposed to be thinking about academics first, but if there is a group of people near you and then there is a book you are supposed to be reading, you are going to choose—it is just so much more easier to go along with the group of people and do what they are doing. And I think a lot of students got caught up in the social life more so than the academics. I was like that my freshman year, but I realized that if I don't go to college there is nothing else for me. And I think a lot of students are like that. It is just an adjustment period, and some people can adjust, and some people—it is going to take them a little while longer.*

*Other students—I don't think they fully know what they want. That is one of failures. Another thing is they don't know how to manage their play. They don't know how to manage their time. I mean, in college—no parents, no guidance. When they are at home they are very structured. In college you have to be centered, individual and independent. A lot of other students—if there is a party going on, "Oh, I'm going to a party." Their priorities aren't set. If things are due that week you got to do it. You got to do your work. They may go out and not do their work, and I think that is part of the failure. I see that with a lot of college students—not just program students. Whereas with me, my work comes first. If I can go out, I will go out. But if I can't, I'm not going to go out, based on goals, and also, based on wants. I mean, you can either be a leader or a follower.*

I have always sought out help. With other people—I think they are intimidated or they are afraid to seek help. I don't see why, because like I said, you are paying them money. And I think some students see their professor as a professor where I see them as a friend. And, like my girlfriend, I will use her as an example—she struggled in a course, and I told her to go seek help. But, she was very hesitant.

I think the reason why some students don't succeed in school or drop out is because they don't appreciate the opportunity that they have. You know, they don't realize what kind of position they are in, what kind of opportunity they could achieve, or what they have and what they can do with their life. They just don't really appreciate life itself, I don't think. They take their lives for granted.

Oh yeah, they _fall_ out of college. College is a big change because you have a lot of free time. You probably have double the amount of free time you do in high school. The whole key to college is just managing your time because a lot of it is wasted. If you don't have a set schedule, it's definitely hard to get motivated. There are a lot of distractions, too.

Some students, um, kind of gave up. There was a student that I came into the program with in 1993, and he was also an athlete. Within a year and a half, he just gave up. He was given study skills from the athletic program and also another program and provided all these extra services that he never took advantage of. The next thing you know he is out of the university. You have to want the help and seek the help, also, in order to get it and benefit from it. Those students who weren't able to succeed, it may have been something else at

174

home or in their personal life that also interacted with their school life. But, at the same time there are people available to talk to—counseling if you need it.

I would say most of the people that have dropped out after the summer that we started here probably just didn't need college to support them or to get them a better job for the rest of their life and didn't take it seriously as a result. I take school seriously because, you know, it gives me some satisfaction to be educated. To be better educated is satisfying enough for me to keep going everyday. Why somebody else didn't take it seriously is hard to know. They may be here because somebody said, "You should be here," I guess.

Some people are innocent victims of just—life. Some people—the burden gets heavy enough, and they make a decision that they are going to put college off for awhile, or they are going to take care of something else they need to take care of in life. Then there are the young and immature that, you know, they want to chase the opposite sex and drink and smoke dope and everything else, you know. You're talking about how much you are working on and they are talking about how much beer they drink. And they last about a year or two, you know. Or the chronic malcontents that aren't always doing well, just picking personality differences of the professors—the blaming types. Or, you know, just—some people have no self-esteem or no sense of work and value. We all have those classes that are brick walls—any profession, I'm sure. When you hit the brick wall, it's like some people crumple up; some people don't.

Some students don't have the support of their families or don't have any supports at all. Some—they just fail to study.

*You still have to study. If all the supports are there, you still have to study. Some people get caught up in the college social life, and that is a big problem why most people don't succeed. They don't learn to balance social life with academics.*

*I think they got caught up in other things, like going out and that. They really didn't have the determination to finish. They didn't have like a long-term goal in mind.*

*Probably because they might have other problems, stuff like—maybe they didn't have any drive or they weren't self-motivators. I think that is a big key too. And not letting yourself get lazy. I mean, it's easy to go home and take a nap every afternoon, but you can't let yourself do that.*

*I think some of them just plainly don't care. I think some of them are doing it because their parents are making them go. I think that is one thing. Another thing—I don't think they have a drive. They feel like, "Okay. I'm failing this class. I can't turn it around. I'm going to quit, or I am just going to fail out. I am not going to give myself the options to, you know, exceed the roadblocks or anything like that." They are just real down on themselves, like they can't do anything. I have gone through that stage where I feel like no matter what I did, I didn't do anything right. They just don't apply themselves. They really don't care. They think they come to college—you always hear—to party—the natural thing. I think they need to have the drive to want to stay in school, to accomplish goals, to set goals first of all. And I feel a lot of students here don't set goals. They don't know what they are here for. They don't know what they are trying to accomplish. I think that you need to have a priority when you get here, and you need to set goals, and you need to try to accomplish them and to do anything you* can to get them. They have their priorities mixed up. Whenever they do get a rude awakening and they are doing bad, some people just feel like, "Oh, I am a loser. I don't need to. I am just stupid." I don't think that anyone is stupid, they just don't have their goals oriented, and I think that is important.

I really don't know what makes them click—some people—the lack of determination, the lack of support, the lack of motivation. I know a lot of people just got tired of college. So, it is a lack of motivation.

I don't think it is ability. I have made two observations. One is that when people come here, like they have led a sheltered life and their parents were pretty strict, and they didn't let them do anything. And, they come here, and they could be gone 3 days at a time, and nobody is going to care, nobody is going to ask. They can go out, and they can do what they want. They can get alcohol anywhere. You can get drugs anywhere. I mean, you can do anything you want, and nobody really cares. And you know, you don't even have to go to class.

I think a lot of people make partying and hanging out with their friends more of a priority than actually doing work.

A lot of people are not ready for school. Some students, you know, they have a good academic foundation. Other students are led to believe, "Hey, you come to college, and you can do exactly what you did in high school." And sometimes during recruiting and everything else you see how different—like for instance—suburban schools—the money that is pumped into those students receiving computers receiving more than adequate, um, professional staff. And then you look at an inner city school. You know, they have a Commodore 64 computer in

*1997. Those things are outdated. Those students come in thinking that their skills are compatible with those that are far more advanced. Here, if you are talking about a minority student, you are talking about culture shock. If you are talking about somebody from one of these small towns, they are at a technological disadvantage.*

*A lot of students—some of them—were born with a silver spoon in their mouth. This is the first time that they have ever had to do anything. Others have their priorities just simply mixed up, you know. Time management is a key, you know. A lot of them waste time.*

Points to Ponder . . .

1. Do you see yourself in any of these descriptions? Do any of the characterizations sounds like you? Have you displayed any of these behaviors or attitudes at some point, but been able to change them or overcome them? If so, why were you able to make the change?

2. Do you disagree with these students' opinions of why some students are not successful in college? Do you have different observations or additional ones? Explain.

3. Pick one of the student excerpts and write a response based on your own experience, observation, and opinion.

4. List all the reasons that are expressed here for failure to succeed. Rate yourself against each of these reasons. Use a scale of low, medium, and high for your ratings. For example, when it comes to

178

setting priorities, how do you rate?  What about being involved in too many social activities or "keeping negative company?"

5.  What have you learned about yourself from doing the above rating exercise?  Are there some areas that you would like to improve?  In other words, if you had a low rating that should have been high, do you need to make some adjustments to optimize your chances of success?  How do you make such adjustments?  Be specific.

## Introduction

Strength of commitment and the importance of a goal were such strong themes in students' descriptions of the college experience, that most gave these factors top priority—along with hard work—when asked what advice they would give new college students about achieving success.  Studies support the concept that goal commitment and an intention to succeed are essential features of a success model, both at the beginning of the integration process into the college experience and at the end of the process.  In other words, given the longitudinal nature of the process, if a student is expected to persist and succeed, the commitment to the goal of success must be retained and reinforced throughout the entire college experience, right up to the end.  It appears that students who participated in this study would agree.  Strength of commitment, or the importance of a goal, was such a strong theme in their descriptions of the successful college experience that they returned to it over and over again, essentially ending with it when asked what advice they would have for other students attending college.

Speaking of Which . . .

*The first thing are your goals.  If you have no reason to be here and you have no goals, then you are wasting your time.*

not a bad thing.  It is just that some people need more time
'evelop a goal.

If you don't want to be here, get lost.  Go find something
to do.

The first thing you have to figure out is why you are
:.  So many people come here, and they have no idea what
· want to do.

Yeah, you are going to have ups and downs, but you need
nd your goal, and you need to set it.

You have to stay focused.  It is so easy to take the easier
When you take the easier road, it just shows that you are
'illing to do what it takes or that you won't.  It doesn't say
you can't.  You just won't.  In today's society you have to
:e that not having a degree doesn't mean you are not the
test person.  Having a degree means you are willing to do
thing maybe a lot of people can't or won't.  There are a lot
nefits to being in college, a lot of benefits to having a
·e.  You have to have personal reasons why you want
'hing for yourself.  I have always felt like I am not here to
degree in order to get a job.  Getting a job to me is kind
k.  Luck is when preparation meets opportunity.  So, I have
'e the preparation in order to meet the opportunity.  Stay
ed.  It is a hard, rough, and rugged road to get what you
But no one said that it would be easy.  Nothing you have
ead from the handouts say it is going to be easy.
ɔne comes up with, "I have this problem."  Sure you will.
'imes things are there to make you better and not bitter.
've to take everything and learn from everything you do.
ᶠ you fail out of college you are closer to getting a degree

182

than a person who never went.  I have always thought every time I failed a physics course, I am closer to being a rocket scientist than the person who did not take that physics course to begin with.

I just want to let individuals know when they come in that you can be successful.  You can do it if you try, you know, and it is not just about grades.  It is about your mentality and your focus and your goals.  If you are goal-oriented and you know you want to succeed and you want a career and you know that there is something out there that you want to do, achieve it.  Strive for it.  Do whatever you have to do.  You will get it.

You'll get it.  You'll get it.  You'll get it.  Just be determined.  Be encouraged, and be committed.  Words of wisdom from a success-failure, success-failure, success-failure, now success again.

I would say not to get down on yourself.  If I was talking to them I would sit them down and say, "Okay.  Let's look at what you did," maybe come up with some ideas of what they could do to benefit themselves and say, "Well, this is just one class, you know.  We can get you back on track, you know.  You have years ahead of you." You could teach them to use some study habits or organization—stuff like that.  Offer them suggestions, and actually make them look at what they did, and maybe help them realize things that they could do to make them more successful.

I would tell students to put forth all their effort, even in the classes that they think that they can't succeed in. Always do your best. You are the only person that knows what you can do. You are the only person that goes through your experiences everyday. Do what you want to do because time goes by so fast. You are just going to look back and say, "I should have done that." If you think you want to do something, just do it. Listen to what other people are saying, you know, but you don't always have to do what they want to do. Listen to what they have to say, even if it is negative. Always listen to the negative stuff, but make your decisions from what you know because you are the only person who can really decide what is best for you.

Be independent. Don't be a follower. Set you goals. Whenever you have things to do, get to it. If there is a party and you have things to do, go with the homework. Do that first. Manage your time. That is like the key factor. And also, know what you want—goal-wise. Do you want a passing grade or do you want an A?

I would just tell them to make the most of their time at school because it does go by fast—real fast. And then get involved in their academics. Find something they're interested in and try to get really involved in that interest academically, and get interested in something outside academics, you know, like a student senate, debate team, whatever. That way you'll meet a lot more people, and you'll make a lot of connections with people that are in your classes too. And it just helps a lot.

I would refer them to the services of a support program. I would like to speak to high school students who are prepared to be entering college and advise them—if they can get into a program then do so. And if not, learn about the learning skills

184

centers at their university because they have numerous resources for you there. A lot of students don't know that. Maybe it is not advertised as much as the athletics and the social clubs and other things like that are. A lot of people think when it is the learning skills center or something to that effect, it is for people who are having difficulty. Or are just dumb. Or have a learning disability. Learning skills centers, and tutoring, and study skills workshops and courses are to help you do better no matter how smart you think you are. A lot of people immediately get defensive, and they say, "I don't need help. I'm fine. I don't have a learning problem." And, it's not that. It's offering you more resources. I would recommend anyone to find out information and to use all your resources.

There are only two things necessary for college, I would tell students. One is a sense of humor and the other one is an umbrella—and that is really all you need to know [laughing]. Seriously, don't take yourself too seriously. If you have a sense of humor—I mean, if you can't laugh about that bad grade like when everyone in the class gets thumped, you're not going to make it. You can get self-obsessed so much that you lose sight of life, and this is just not a part of it. You're not going to be very happy. And if you aren't very happy, then you are not going to stay.

Find a support, especially if you live far away. Find someone that you really depend on, that you can call—not an acquaintance, but somebody you can really trust, someone who is going to tell you, "Look, you don't need to go there. I have been here long enough to know what places you should and should not go to. I mean, if you want to go that is up to you. I'm going to let you know what happened at that place." New students—I find they really need like a mentor, somebody in their field who has been here for some time to give them the in's and out's so they don't have to go through the bumps and the scratches that you did trying to get through. It is okay if you make a mistake, but realize you have to pay for those mistakes that you make. Go through and really analyze before you really do anything.

I would tell like a class of high school seniors, "Go to college if you want to, but if you don't, don't do it." I mean, it isn't a must that you have to go to college to be successful.

I would tell students not to give up—that no matter how bad it seems, you can always turn things around. If you are in a major that you are not comfortable in—look for another one that you will be more comfortable in, that you will have more success in. If you are having emotional problems or problems within yourself—go see somebody. There are so many resources out there for you to use. But if you don't go and try to find them, then you are not really going to accomplish anything. Yeah, you are going to have ups and downs. You need to get on that road. I think that is really important, and what people have got to realize is that they need to <u>set</u> a goal first and then try to accomplish it.

First thing I always say to new students is, "Look, read." Do your assignments. Just get the assignment read because the fact of the matter is, if you don't read for class—because you have reading for every class—it doesn't matter what it is and it is always too much—read. Some people like to go to class and then read afterwards. I found it better to be prepared for class, and then you can read it again if you have to or outline it afterwards. And go to class.

I would tell them the first thing they have to c
out why they are here.  So many people come here an
have no idea what they want to do.  That is the first :
they are here and what they want to get out of being
then once they know that, they have to prioritize.

I would say, "Those who think they can, they w.
who think they can't, they won't"—and in order to be .
it does not necessarily mean how many times that you
it means how many times you pick yourself up.  Draw :
from what brought you down and finish that particula
Finish the program or whatever you start.  Don't let c
get the best of you because your life is a gift from G
what you make of it is a gift from Him.  If you apply ;
you know, everybody can make it.  You can make it.  Y
some of it is harder because you have to jump a few .
hurdles.  So you may not finish in the same time that
person finishes, but after awhile you begin to get qu
at the end of the race you see that you ran a lot fas;
that other person because your legs are stronger fr
those hurdles.

Points to Ponder . . .

1.  If you were given an opportunity to give advice to other
    about how to be successful in college and how to get the
    the experience, what would you tell them?

2.  If you were asked to tell entering freshmen what pitfal
    what would you say?

3. Make a list of one-liner "Tips and Advice to Other Students." Your statements can be as general as "Be an active not passive learner" or as specific as "Get A's in your easy classes." Feel free to borrow from the statements you have read throughout this book. Have others in your class or group add items to your list.

4. Think of ways to make your list available to others that might benefit. Brainstorm ideas about distribution or publication with your classmates.